(*Continued from front flap*)

ment, perhaps Barth's most significant theological accomplishment was his exposition of Anselm's theological method. The influence of Anselm may be seen not only in the method and style of the *Dogmatics*, but also in the form of Barth's resistance to Nazism (when he *did* make headlines: *Dr. Karl Barth Arrested in Germany*).

Karl Barth has been described as incontestably the greatest figure in Christian theology to appear for decades; as the greatest dogmatic theologian since Thomas Aquinas; as a man determined to be a theologian of the Word of God. This short, insightful account provides new understandings of both the man and his work.

T. H. L. Parker received his D.D. from Cambridge University. He is a Church of England clergyman who has spent most of his thirty years' ministry in country parishes. Presently he is Vicar of Oakington, a village near Cambridge. The author has translated part of the *Church Dogmatics* into English, and was one of the two assistant editors of the work. He edited the British *Festschrift* for Barth's seventieth birthday, *Essays in Christology* for Karl Barth, and was joint editor with Dr. J. I. McCord of the American-British tribute on Barth's eightieth birthday, *Service in Christ*. He has written, translated, or edited over a dozen books on the Reformation and on Karl Barth.

Karl Barth

by

T. H. L. PARKER

William B. Eerdmans Publishing Company
Grand Rapids, Michigan

Foreword

It will be as well if I say at the outset that almost all my acquaintance with Karl Barth lay through his books. Personal knowledge of him I had practically none, for I met him on only three occasions. Most of the afternoon and evening of July 4, 1956, I spent in his company. This was when he was presented by the Archbishop of Canterbury with a book in honour of his seventieth birthday. A few days later I chatted with him and his son, Markus Barth, on the platform of Grantham railway station — at least, I was on the platform and they were in the *Flying Scotsman,* bound for London from Edinburgh. Then in July 1960 Barth and his secretary entertained my wife and me one evening in his study in Basel.

Obviously this does not add up to very much; certainly not enough to be able to write of him from personal experience. I have never studied under him, never even heard him lecture or preach (except once on the wireless in English about 1947). If one does not know the subject of a biography personally, one has to get to know him in other ways. With great figures in the past this is usually not too difficult. There will be available documentary evidence in the form of earlier lives and, most important of all, letters to and from him. But I began this book while Barth was still happily with us, and so no complete biography existed. Of letters there was only the collection entitled *Revolutionary Theology in the Making,* the correspondence between Barth and Thurneysen. Immensely valuable as this was, it was material that had to be used with caution. There was little to check it by, nor other letters that might present a somewhat different aspect. Also unhappily it stopped in 1925, so that I was like a hitch-hiker whose kindly host had to set him down at a point short of his destination, to find his way alone. For the rest I had to make do with such scraps of information as I could assemble. Barth's three articles in *How I Changed My Mind* were useful as pointers, but they were not sufficiently detailed. The period of the German Church conflict was well documented, however, and here I could rely on the official histories and newspaper accounts.

When all was said and done, there were still quite a few puzzles, incidents that did not make sense, inconsistencies between apparently authenticated facts, and so on. For clearing up some of these puzzles I am more grateful than I can say, first of all, to Dr. Eduard Thurneysen, who replied most fully to many questions that I asked him, and was able to correct some mistaken impressions. Quite possibly there are still a lot of things, especially about the early days, that he will think I have got wrong, but I hope not. Other puzzles were explained for me most kindly by Professor Markus Barth and by Dr. Eberhard Busch, Karl Barth's secretary at the last. I should again make clear that it is I who am responsible for the view of Barth presented in the book.

The reader will soon see what sort of a biography this is, less an account of Barth's life than of his thought and his writings. It is not addressed to those who are already learned in Barth, but to students — by whom I mean those who know little or nothing about him and would like to remedy matters. There is no dedication in the usual place, because the list of dedicatees would be a long one. I offer it to all my friends over many years at Lincoln Theological College who used to accompany me through the history and theology of the Reformation until, in two final lectures on Karl Barth, we would view the landskip o'er. And with them my friends of more recent years at Westcott House, Cambridge, remembering some happy hours of lectures and seminars on Barth and especially a good and pleasant (at least for me) week in July 1964. Quite a few explanations in this book come from criticisms and awkward questions that arose in seminars, and some who took part will see that I was not insensitive to what they said.

My chief thanks must be given to my wife for the considerable work that she did in typing and general secretarial tidying up.

T. H. L. PARKER

Contents

Abbreviations

Most of the references to books will be easily understood, even where I have not given the full title. The only ones that might be obscure are:

Dialectic Theology = *The Beginnings of Dialectic Theology* (edited by J. M. Robinson. John Knox Press, 1968).

How I Changed = Karl Barth: *How I Changed My Mind* (edited by J. D. Godsey. John Knox Press, 1966).

Natural Theology = *Natural Theology. Comprising Nature and Grace by Professor Dr. Emil Brunner and the reply "No!" by Dr. Karl Barth* (translated by P. Fraenkel. Geoffrey Bles, 1946).

Rev. Theol. = *Revolutionary Theology in the Making.* Barth-Thurneysen Correspondence, 1914-1925 (translated by J. D. Smart. John Knox Press 1964, Epworth Press 1964).

I am grateful to the John Knox Press and the Epworth Press for permission to quote this last book extensively.

CHAPTER ONE

The Road to the Desert

1

THE ROAD TO THE DESERT RAN THROUGH CENTRAL SWITZERLAND. It lay, as a sort of theological intersection, on what was Route Number 5 in the 1897 Baedeker.

> *From Bâle to Lucerne.* 59 M. Railway in 2-4 hrs. (fares 10fr.25, 7fr.15, 5fr.20c.)
>
> To (27 M.) *Aarburg,* the junction for *Bern* (see p. 17). The Lucerne line traverses the broad grassy *Wiggerthal.*
>
> 30 M. *Zofingen* (1430'; pop. 4496; *Rössli; Ochs),* a busy little town. The library in the Town Hall contains coins, autographs of Swiss reformers, and the album of a society of artists, founded in 1806, which formerly met at Zofingen. On the branches of the fine old lime-trees near the *Schützenhaus* are two 'ball-rooms'. In the *Bleichegut,* near the town, are the remains of a Roman bath.
>
> From Zofingen to Suhr, railway in 36 minutes. Stations *Safenwyl, Kölliken, Entfelden,* well-to-do villages, and (10½ M.) *Suhr,* the junction for Aarau and Baden (p. 22).

But to follow our old Baedeker on to Kölliken and Entfelden, those other well-to-do villages, and above all to (10½ M.) Suhr, would be going too far. We alight at the sizeable village of Safenwil. Our interest, however, does not lie in its light industries or farming, but in the pastor, an unusual man, at this time some thirty years old. His photograph must surely belie him. The drooping moustache, short-cropt hair, the pince-nez spectacles on their gold chain, and especially the tall stiff collar, combine to present the profile of one who would not be out of place as a respectable and bourgeois character in Ibsen or George Bernard Shaw, a pillar of society. The pastor, however, was far from being a pillar of the established order. Not only was he a member of the Social Democratic Party fighting the cause of women workers in the local knitting factory; he was also telling his hearers in sermons and addresses that the god of the Western world was finished: 'He is not even righteous. He cannot prevent

9

his worshippers, all the distinguished European and American apostles of civilization, welfare, and progress, all zealous citizens and pious Christians, from falling upon one another with fire and sword to the amazement and derision of the poor heathen in India and Africa. This god is really an unrighteous god, and it is high time for us to become thorough-going doubters, sceptics, scoffers, and yes, even atheists, in regard to him. It is high time for us to confess openly and gladly that this god, to whom we have built the tower of Babel, is not God. He is an idol. He is dead' *(Word of God and Word of Man,* p. 22). The pastor had begun to write a book that was destined to disable the settled thinking of the Western Churches. For the 1897 Baedeker Safenwil may have been just a well-to-do village on the line from Zofingen to Suhr, but in 1916 it deserved rather more attention as the nursery of modern theology.

Karl Barth had gone there in 1911, at the age of twenty-five, after being assistant minister in the German-speaking church at Geneva, which in those days used to meet under the shadow of the cathedral in the *Auditoire*, the lecture room of Calvin. Like any good young minister, he took his duties at Safenwil seriously. He was uncomfortably conscious of his responsibility towards the village and its inhabitants, a responsibility that was certainly not exhausted, but yet concentrated, in the sermons to be preached on a Sunday. Church law and social custom demanded sermons as the centre of the congregational worship. But if sermons were considered with a cool and secular eye, they took on a strange and questionable appearance. What was the preacher supposed to tell his congregation? Why was he supposed to do this? He was meant to teach people about God; but by what right could he claim to possess the knowledge of this ultimate mystery? 'He will open the Bible and read from it words of infinite import, words that all relate to God. And then he will climb up into the pulpit and — what daring for any man! — preach, that is, add to what has been read from the Bible something from his own head and heart; for one it will be thoughts as Biblical as his knowledge and conscience can make them, for another thoughts which fly daringly or nervously beyond the Bible. On Saturday the one prepared a "conservative" sermon, the other a "liberal"; but does it matter much, in view of the Object? It seems that everyone must, may be *nolens volens*, talk about God' (*Word of God and Word of Man*, p. 106).

Barth's dilemma was not perhaps, as he himself imagined, the fault of his training, but its result. He saw himself as one who had been trained for one activity but forced in the event to undertake another. 'Like all of you, I was a minister and possessed my theology — although, of course, it was not my own but that of my unforgotten teacher Wilhelm Herrmann grafted on to the Reformed principles which I had assimilated almost unconsciously at home . . . . Quite apart from my theological habits of thought, I was pushed ever more strongly by all sorts of circumstances on to the specific problem of the minister, his preaching' (*Word of God and Word of Man*, p. 100). This is not quite accurate. It was what Barth learned at home and at university that was shaped by the problem he encountered as a minister.

The form of words is advised. Not so much what Barth was taught as what he learned. For here we must quite abandon the literary device of understatement and come boldly out into the open. We are not writing the story of one who became a theologian somewhat late in life — say, at the age of thirty — after having passed his formative years in some other pursuit, of one who was an amateur theologian, to be classed by the professionals as a prophet, a poet, or a preacher. It was not the writing of his commentary on Romans nor the preparation of his professorial lectures that made him a theologian. If there is truth in the often repeated praises of him, that his is a "beautiful theology", that he is "incontestably the greatest figure in Christian theology that has appeared for decades", that, most boldly and from, reputedly, a Pope, he is the greatest dogmatic theologian since St Thomas Aquinas, then we cannot believe that this man of genius was born in or about 1916. The qualities that distinguish the professor at Basel are already plain to be marked in the pastor of Safenwil, even in the undergraduate in Bern, Berlin, Tübingen and Marburg. Not the least of these qualities is that which is the unmistakable sign of the preëminent intellect, the faculty of assimilation and rejection, of being ready to learn,

and yet of being capable of choosing from what is heard. He
can himself put it quite bluntly: 'I let Herrmann say to me . . . .'
It is most clearly apparent in his relationship to Wilhelm Herrmann, but it is also true of his home upbringing.

For Barth had been, so to say, a theologian from his birth,
even if in his early years by proxy. His father was at that time
lecturer at a college in Basel, but three years later moved to
Bern, where he became first, Lecturer, and later, Professor in
New Testament and Church History. Fritz Barth was not one of
the famous nineteenth century theological figures, but he was a
competent representative of the more conservative sort of Reformed theologian. Karl Barth began his theological training at
Bern under his father, but the reading of Immanuel Kant gave
him a desire to study under one of the leading exponents of
Kant, Wilhelm Herrmann at Marburg. It seems that his father
distrusted Herrmann's theology, and persuaded him to go to Berlin under the famous Adolf Harnack. Barth sighed as a theologian and obeyed as a son.

Harnack had been a pupil of Albrecht Ritschl, and had
accepted his general view that faith is not to be conceived as
assent to metaphysical doctrines about God but as adherence to
the person of the historical Jesus. A few years before Barth went
to Berlin, Harnack had delivered his famous course of lectures
which were published under the title *What Is Christianity?* In the
opening lecture he had said: 'But the point of view of the philosophical theorist, in the strict sense of the word, will also find no
place in these lectures . . . . We shall keep to the purely historical
theme. What is the Christian religion? Where are we to look for
our materials? The answer seems to be simple and at the same
time exhaustive: *Jesus Christ and his Gospel*' (p. 19). It was as
the exponent of a theology based on the man Jesus, as a Church
historian so encyclopaedic in learning and ready of mind that
(as I have been told by one of his pupils) he wrote all his great
historical works without notes, and as ambassador of the Weimar
Republic in Washington, that Harnack became famous. Barth
spent the year 1906-1907 under him. Even after this, however,
he did not proceed at once to Marburg and Herrmann. Instead
he studied at Tübingen under the New Testament scholar Adolf

Schlatter. Only then was he free to follow his wishes. Yet he had been learning from Herrmann even as a student of Harnack. In the year 1906 he read Herrmann's *Ethik*, published five years earlier — and became a theologian: 'Herrmann was *the* theological teacher of my student years. The day twenty years ago in Berlin when I first read his *Ethik* I remember as if it were today. . . . I can say that on that day I believe my own deep interest in theology began' (*Theology and Church*, p. 238). The place that Barth gives Herrmann as the chief influence of his life must make us spend a little time talking about him.

Herrmann, the son of a country minister, was born in 1846, and so belonged to the generation that was exposed to the full blast of nineteenth century destructive rationalism. He was fortunate, however, in becoming the protégé of Friedrich August Tholuck, a man little enough remembered today, save by specialists, but who was thought so highly of at the turn of the century as to be given no less than seven full pages in Hauck's *Realencyklopädie*; even "Thomas von Aquino" who comes soon after him gets only thirteen. Tholuck was already sixty-seven when Herrmann began his undergraduate career at Halle in 1866. As he was in need of an amanuensis, Herrmann went to live with him in that capacity in 1867. Tholuck was a middle of the way evangelical, a man of piety and a great supporter of Eastern missions; as a scholar he is chiefly memorable for his advocacy of the theology of the Reformers and for his editions of Calvin's *Institutio* and New Testament Commentaries. He himself wrote a commentary on Romans. Herrmann lived familiarly with Tholuck for three years. He was then away from Halle for a few years but returned as Privat-Docent in 1874. Tholuck was still alive and it was at his house that Herrmann met Ritschl, whom he had previously known only through his writings. He was soon a convinced Ritschlian, although perhaps he imported into Ritschl's theology a quality which not a little transformed its character. In 1879 he became Professor of Systematic Theology at Marburg, and remained there until his death in 1922.

It is clear that the mature Barth has had little use for Ritschl. It was only a tired generation, he said in the *Church Dogmatics*, which could see a gleam of hope in Ritschl's theology. What then could the theology of the Ritschlian Wilhelm Herrmann offer him? The answer must be partly in the quality that Herrmann imported into Ritschlianism, and partly in one particular line in it. Ritschl's basic programme was to approach the New Testament by way of the Reformation. Such an aim no doubt appealed to Herrmann, but as a disciple of Tholuck he had no need to be taught the importance of the Reformation. Nor did Barth in his turn learn this lesson from Herrmann. But Ritschl also emphasized the objective character of Christian faith. Faith is based on the revelation of God in the Jesus Christ of the New Testament, and therefore, correspondingly, against Schleiermacher, theology must not become a description of the movements of the mind of the believer. Ritschl carried this so far as to give his numerous enemies the opportunity of jibing at his lack of piety and religion. Herrmann interpreted him more kindly as a man who hated sentimentality and insincere religious talk: 'He observed in religious intercourse an extraordinary strictness with himself. That he lived in the world of ideas contained in the Christian faith, certainly made itself so strongly felt in his conversation that a less powerful intellect was apt to become tired with it. In his house and here in Marburg I have been with him for days on end without his once breaking, by a lighter conversation of any length, his preoccupation with higher things. One saw in this how deeply these matters had taken hold of him. But seldom did he utter a weak or sentimental word. Sharply and exactly he spoke of what moved his heart . . . . There are people endowed with a wonderful facility in religious discourse. Towards the gift of such people Ritschl was in the highest degree susceptible . . . . All the more painful did he feel it when religious talk, which ventured to touch what is highest, struck him as artificial. He treated the professionals in this sphere as his deadly enemies. They have paid him back richly in kind' (*Faith and Morals*, pp. 16-17).

When Herrmann goes on to say that 'Ritschl . . . treated this evil habit in individual instances as a profanation of the holiest' (p. 17), we hear the distinctive note of his theology, the quality that transformed what he learned from Ritschl, and that made him in due course Barth's teacher *par excellence*.

Faith is objective; its object is the historical Jesus in whom God reveals himself; it is an activity of the whole person, showing itself in his outward life. Certainly. But for Herrmann this objective faith reveres and adores the mystery of God in Christ. It is easy to see why Barth was dissatisfied with the confessionalism that lives on the faith of the Reformers, with the correct New Testament theology of the more conservative scholars, and with the shallower and somewhat glib Ritschlianism of Harnack, and listened so joyfully to the voice of Herrmann's faith, so living, so profound, yet so human. 'I let Herrmann say to me one essential truth. This truth, followed out to its consequences, later forced me to say almost everything else quite differently and finally led me even to an interpretation of the fundamental truth itself which was entirely different from his. And yet it was *he* who showed me that truth' (*Theology and Church*, p. 239). The truth was this fundamental quality that transformed Herrmann's Ritschlianism. Barth had heard in his lectures: 'The religious knowledge of the Christian begins with the group of obvious facts establishing religion's power to affect conscience, but it ends with the confession that the God whose innermost nature has become revealed to us as love, still remains for us a God enthroned in unapproachable light (I Timothy 6.16). The doctrine of the Trinity has therefore supreme significance because it reminds us that God who gives us eternal life through himself must be inexhaustible and therefore an unfathomable mystery' (*Theology and Church*, pp. 253f.). God preserves his hiddenness even in his revelation. The most objectionable feature of conservative theology, its blatant or concealed claim to be on such familiar terms with God, to possess him, to be fellow directors with him in the Divine company, is made impossible by this simple truth.

Not that Herrmann deliberately intended by "revelation", by "Christ", or perhaps even by "God", what his pupil came later to mean. Barth has analyzed Herrmann's theology in an essay of 1925 called *The Principles of Dogmatics according to Wilhelm Herrmann*. He shows how inconsistent this truth is with Herrmann's declared intentions and also how he himself received it as his own and allowed it to shape his thought. To the young

Barth emerging from the university, however, it remained only as an irritant, while he attached himself "with passable conviction" to the Ritschlian historicism of Herrmann and Harnack. It seemed like a happy omen when the postman brought him, a few minutes before he was to preach his first sermon in Geneva, the gift from Herrmann of the fourth edition of his *Ethik*.

It was indeed a happy omen. He had been drawn to Herrmann by the question of ethics; he saw that his teachers were men who were concerned for the life of the world; he himself was not content to be an inward Christian only. Thus, their position and his stood and fell by ethical integrity. Before he had been three years in Safenwil, Christianized Europe had started the most deadly of wars. Cultured Germany, liberal England and civilized France were fighting together like mad animals. And hardly had the war begun than Barth's theological teachers joined with others in declaring their support for the Kaiser: 'One day in early August 1914 stands out in my personal memory as a black day. Ninety-three German intellectuals impressed public opinion by their proclamation in support of the war policy of Wilhelm II and his counsellors. Among these intellectuals I discovered to my horror almost all of my theological teachers whom I had greatly venerated. In despair over what this indicated about the signs of the time, I suddenly realized that I could not any longer follow either their ethics and dogmatics or their understanding of the Bible and history. For me at least, nineteenth century theology no longer held any future' (*Humanity of God*, p. 14). Among the names stood those of Gustav-Adolf v. Harnack, Director General of the "Royal Library" and Professor of Church History in Berlin, Reinhold Seeberg, Professor of Theology in Berlin, Adolf Schlatter, Professor of New Testament Exegesis in Tübingen, and, the crowning stroke, Wilhelm Herrmann, Professor of Theology in the University of Marburg.

Why was this incident, easily explicable as a symptom of early war fever, of such decisive importance for Barth? Because neo-Protestantism was a German phenomenon. This movement spread to other lands, it even had shadowy contemporary analogues in other lands, but in its original and pure form it was

German, springing from the cultured Schleiermacher, the learned Ritschl. This neo-Protestantism was Barth's form of religion. But now it was proclaiming itself as nationalistic, as bound to a particular culture, by such terrifying statements as: 'It is not true that the war against our so-called militarism is not also a war against our culture, as our enemies hypocritically claim. Without German militarism, German culture would long since have perished from the earth' (*L'Appel*, p. 54), or: 'Believe us! Believe that we shall fight this war to the end as a civilized race, to whom the heritage of a Goethe, a Beethoven, a Kant, is no less holy than its hearth and its soil' (p. 56). Neo-Protestantism allied itself to these statements and so unmasked itself as a religion sprung from a culture and bound to a culture. When Barth recognized the true character of his religion, he was finished with it.

2

Yet, as Augustine said in the *De Civitate Dei*, you have only lost everything when you have lost faith. Barth did not become a cynic, a sceptic or a religious anarchist. The building had collapsed, the foundations were shaken. He set to work to excavate the foundations and lay fresh ones. The dogmatics that sprang from a moral attachment to the supreme man Jesus and proclaimed this as faith in the revelation of God had been unmasked. It remained to be discovered what these words "faith", "revelation", and "God" really meant.

At this time, he was grappling with the problem and activity of preaching. The preacher was to talk about God; he was to exhort his congregation to believe in God. But the word "God" had become exhausted of meaning. 'It is high time for us to become thorough-going doubters, sceptics, scoffers, and yes, even atheists, in regard to him. It is high time for us to confess openly and gladly that this god, to whom we have built the tower of Babel, is not God. He is an idol. He is dead' (*Word of God and Word of Man*, p. 22).

What Barth's course would have been if he had had to tread it alone, who can tell? But in the summer of 1913 the village of Leutwil, eight or nine miles away to the east, gained a new minister, by name Eduard Thurneysen. Barth and Thurneysen were not strangers, for they had met in Marburg in 1908. Their course had been so far not dissimilar. Thurneysen also was a native of Basel, and it was there that he began his theological studies. His two leading teachers were the Church historian Paul Wernle and the Old Testament scholar Bernard Duhm, each internationally famous in his own field of study. From Basel Thurneysen went to Marburg for two semesters in 1908-9 and sat under Jülicher, the New Testament scholar, and Wilhelm Herrmann. Now it was that he met Barth, who was spending a year as assistant to Martin Rade, the editor of *Christliche Welt*, the leading German liberal periodical. Thurneysen returned to Basel in 1909 and finished off his studies there before spending a year as secretary of what we might call the Student Christian Movement in Zürich.

That Thurneysen moved to a parish so close to Barth's was quite unintentional. 'I think it was a divine leading. For how else could we have been able so completely to coordinate our theological work?' (Thurneysen, Private Letter). But now there developed a relationship perhaps unique in the history of theology. Masters and pupils, or collaborators in a specific task, can be found in abundance. But for two men to be in such accord without either surrendering his individuality and independence is surely most rare. In such accord that they could publish joint volumes of sermons without indication of authorship; and yet so distinct that the one could naturally find his way into the academic world and the other just as naturally pursue his pastoral course and his theological interest in literature until in middle age he combined his ministry at the Basel Münster with a professorship of practical theology at the university. In this friendship there was no junior partner. It was together that they sought to clear the ground and lay fresh foundations. 'We were both convinced that *new ways* had to be sought in theology' (Thurneysen, Private Letter). And this meant that they sought together to understand the formal basis of the Christian faith, the Bible. They were frequently in each other's house, sitting day-long in talk; they preached in each other's church; they carried on a regular and full correspondence. And very early they were aware that they had reached an understanding of the faith that was distinctive and new in their time. Barth could speak in letters of 1915 of "our essential orientation", of "our cause", of the "new world" that they had entered. He begins to look back with detachment on his undergraduate days, tracing his fresh insights to their source, hailing some of his student thoughts with friendly recognition. He has now become "frightfully indifferent" about "the purely historical questions". 'Of course, that is nothing new for me. Already under the influence of Herrmann, I always thought of historical criticism as merely a means of attaining freedom in relation to the tradition, not, however, as a constituent factor in a new liberal tradition' (*Rev. Theol.* p. 36). And at the same time the two revolutionaries, conscious of their separateness but not without some self-directed humour, prepare for the day when they will 'strike the great blow against the theologians' (*Rev. Theol.* p. 36).

Now everything became suspect. Pietism and hot gospelling had never been attractive. Ritschlianism and Western culture were early victims in this theological purge. But then one evening at Leutwil the opinion long felt was at last spoken: they could not go along with Schleiermacher. The two Protestant pastors stood outside Protestantism, unable to belong to any ecclesiastical or theological group or school. They had taken "the road to the desert", leaving behind them 'so much beloved trash, so many dear illusions and practical, all too practical, naivetes, that they [found] themselves freezing afterwards and [knew] not where to turn for shelter' (*Theology and Church*, p. 57).

The theology in which they had been educated had been found wanting ethically, as a guide and stay in the time of the breaking of the nations. It proved no more help to men laden with the intolerable yoke of preaching. Their training had been directed towards the acquisition of the knowledge of certain technical skills — the history of the Church, the history of dogma, ethics, philosophy, psychology, dogmatics, pastoralia. The preaching that the ordinands would be called upon to do was by no means forgotten. They were taught that this was a difficult task, to fulfil which they ought to pray for the help of God. A difficult task, but not impossible. But while he was only twenty-

three Barth had voiced his worry about this situation in the periodical *Zeitschrift für Theologie und Kirche*. Why, he asked, is
there less impulse towards foreign mission work among the
products of "modernist" theological faculties? This needs to be
asked, because it is only a part of a wider problem: 'It is far
more difficult to undertake activity in the pulpit, at the sick-bed,
or in the clubhouse, if you are an alumnus of Marburg or Heidelberg rather than of Halle or Greifswald' (p. 317). And the
longer he engaged in the preaching office, the more bewildered
he became. Perhaps there was something wrong with him personally, so that what was an enigma to him was clear to everyone
else? Observation of other ministers failed to support this view;
the fact remained that preaching seemed not merely difficult but
impossible, and that he was conscious only of the pressure, of
the *Not*, the lack and distressful necessity, of preaching.

They turned to the Bible. 'We decided we had to read the
New Testament a little differently from and more exactly than
our teachers,' said Thurneysen (*Rev. Theol.* p. 75). This is
more accurate than Barth's description of the same event, that
together they had read the Bible without presuppositions. Such a
psychological feat would be beyond achievement. It is clear
that what they set out to do was to listen to the voice of the
Bible without being distracted or influenced by the voice of the
Protestant tradition of the nineteenth century. By turning to the
Bible, they "were converted to the Bible", to its point of view
and its authority. Their difference from their teachers did not
lie primarily in a different exegesis, but more fundamentally in
a difference of approach. No longer for them the principles of
interpretation that they had learnt at Berlin and Marburg, according to which the Bible is to be treated in two separate ways,
historically and devotionally. Historically, in that it was to serve
as the object of historical research. From this point of view a
scholar could engage in the study of the Bible with no more
personal implication than, say, A. E. Housman experienced in
editing the Latin astronomer-poet Manilius. On the other hand,
whether for Schleiermacher or Ritschl or Harnack, this book
was, in one way or another, the foundation of Christianity and
the source from which Christians drew their spiritual life. It is

therefore also to be read spiritually or devotionally. This duality, impossible to dissolve because the principles that posited it were fundamental in these theological systems, was to be seen reflected in the custom among some English ordinands in the late nineteen-thirties of possessing two Bibles, in one of which they could mark with coloured pencils such things as the strata of J and E in Genesis, while the other could be read in their times of devotion.

There is a fault here graver than over-enthusiasm needing to be corrected by a steady comprehensiveness. What was at stake was the historical basis of the Christian faith. When, for Schleiermacher, the centre of Christianity became an individual Christian's experience of the divine and his faith in the 'Christ' who had a perfect awareness of God, instead of events in history, of what Jesus Christ did and what happened to him, it was impossible that the New Testament should be treated as the record and interpretation of those events. When, on the other hand, for Ritschl's pupil Harnack, the centre of gravity shifts on to the Jesus of history, it is only apparently that Schleiermacher has been corrected. For the historical method which Harnack, like most of his contemporaries, employed demanded an impartiality towards the subject of enquiry. But the Christian's attitude to Christ and the New Testament is most certainly not one of impartiality but of faith. History and faith are again set at loggerheads. History is victorious, and for faith is substituted a mystical attachment to Jesus, the divine teacher, the supreme leader and spiritual hero.

The study of the Bible was therefore pursued under the guidance of these two impulses. It was read devotionally for the good of the soul. And it was subjected to a more thorough and pitiless historical and literary criticism than any other documents have ever undergone. The individual books were treated simply as literary specimens or historical and sociological quarries. Their authorship and dates were carefully investigated. The life and religion of the Jews at the various stages of their history were studied as a part of the general history of the Middle East. The thought of the writers of the New Testament, not to mention their psychology, was searched into and related. All the talk was of the growth of monotheism in the Old Testament, of the conflict of the prophets with the priestly cult in Israel, of the "historicity" of the Gospels with special reference to the "Synoptic problem" and the "Johannine problem", of the influence of St Paul's "experience" on the Damascus road upon his theology, of the conflict between Jesus and Paul.

One would have thought that the consequence of this almost exclusive occupation with the historical would have been plain from the beginning. Far from bringing the Bible nearer to modern man, the effect of the historical method was to remove it ever further and further away, so that the next step was the attempt to counter-act this movement by writing books and articles on the "relevance" of the Bible, or Isaiah, or Jesus, or Paul, for today.

Of course, the historical method did not have things all its own way. A quite formidable body of conservative or positive theologians fought every inch of the ground. Yet, although they were equally learned with their opponents, and indeed would be adjudged correct in some of their views by a later and more dispassionate assessment, they were doomed to defeat, not only because the tide was running strongly against them, but also because they attempted to defend the indefensible. They were unable to put forward firmly and clearly a satisfactory alternative to the historical method, and they were unable to prove that this method led to insecure results. Barth's father was not untypical with his book on the life and teaching of Jesus: *Die Hauptprobleme des Lebens Jesu*. Moderate, pious and scholarly, it attempts to show that in fact the Synoptic Gospels do not support the "liberal" view of Jesus. The work must have been quite well received by those whose faith needed academic support, for it went into three editions between 1899 and 1907. It would seem that the early influence of his father helped to prevent Barth from becoming a whole-hearted Ritschlian even in his university days, and it was no empty tribute that the preface to the first edition of *The Epistle to the Romans* paid: 'The understanding of history is an uninterrupted conversation between the wisdom of yesterday and the wisdom of tomorrow. And it is a conversation always conducted honestly and with discernment.

In this connexion I cannot fail to think with gratitude and re-spect of my father, Professor Fritz Barth. For such discernment he signally displayed throughout his whole active life' (p. 1). To this influence was added Herrmann's authoritative voice saying: 'Historical research cannot confront us with the Saviour Jesus Christ. It cannot help us to find the historical Christ whom Christians assert to be their salvation' (quoted in *Theology and Church*, p. 250). The way was therefore to some extent pre-pared for reading the Bible "a little bit differently."

In the autumn of 1916 Barth gave a simple lecture in Thurneysen's church at Leutwil: 'The New World in the Bible'. Here, with the thrilling voice of discovery, he spoke of the Bible which had disclosed itself to them. What is in the Bible? The Bible is full of history of every kind, but the history it records creates historical difficulties, for it places the causes of great events outside history. In a popular manner, suited to his village audience, Barth was saying that the law of cause and effect on which the historical method depended was not the law by which the Biblical writers operated. For them the cause was God acting in the world. When God acts, history according to the Renais-sance and Enlightenment understanding ceases to exist and a new and different sort of history begins, 'a history with its own dis-tinct grounds, possibilities and presuppositions' (*Word of God and Word of Man*, p. 37).

Again, the Bible contains moral teaching, and this is, in general, of a lofty nature. Yet the example of some of the Biblical heroes is hardly to be imitated — Abraham's slaying of Isaac, Jacob's deceit, Elijah's slaughter of the priests. Nor does the Bible contain clear and unambiguous instruction on a host of ethical problems that bewilder modern man. This is not its purpose. It relates, not the exemplary acts of mankind but the praiseworthy acts of God as he establishes his new world. And the hero of the Bible is not the moral man but the sinner: 'Into this world the publicans and the harlots will go before your im-peccably elegant and righteous folk of good morality' (p. 40).

Yet, again, the Bible is a manifestation of true religion. It teaches the truth about God and shows how he is to be found and what service he demands of man. This is correct, even if the various Christian 'religions' all appeal to the Bible in justification of their existence. But the real content of the Bible is not a setting forth of the true religion by which men may attain to God and serve him, but rather the declaration of God's "thoughts about men": 'The Bible tells us not how we should talk with God but what he says to us; not how we find the way to him, but how he has sought and found the way to us' (p. 43).

The new world in the Bible is the world of God, his sovereignty, his glory, his incomprehensible love. But whom are we speaking about? Who is this God? He is not the God of pietism, with its chosen few, its inward peace, and its other-worldly hope. The Bible does not exist so that 'here and there specimens of men like you and me might be "converted", find inner "peace", and by a redeeming death go some day to "heaven" ' (p. 47). God plans a greater thing than that, nothing less than the establishment of a new world; Jesus Christ is the redeemer of all mankind, of sinful mankind, of all creation; the Holy Spirit makes all things new, "new men, new families, new relationships, new politics"; he establishes God's righteousness in the midst of man's unrighteousness and will not cease his work until everything dead is quickened and a new world exists.

This simple lecture (which is not, however, always well expressed) is one of the most important of Barth's early statements. Already there lies within it in embryo the whole basis of the *Church Dogmatics*. Moreover, it shows in a clear and even masterly way his break from nineteenth century theology. But also there are to be seen clearly the lights that illuminated the Bible for Barth and Thurneysen. They were reading, no doubt among much else, Kierkegaard and Dostoevsky. Kierkegaard, a man compact of contradictions, a pitiless hater of established Christianity and yet a thinker who trod willingly the traditional paths of theology, one who opposed sentimentality and humbug with a clear and stern reasoning and yet whose books emerged out of the unhappy circumstances and bewilderments of his personal life, was one whom no theologian could once take seriously and then return to his former course. No longer could he mistake Religion A for Religion B, let alone attempt to combine them or to pass off the one as the other. And he must be a dull fellow indeed whose reading of Kierkegaard does not give a bite to his theological style. Kierkegaard may justly be called the father of modern theology: perhaps Barth must even share with him the credit for *The Epistle to the Romans* and the *Church Dogmatics*. Already in 1846, occupied with the problem of 'contemporaneity', Kierkegaard was attacking the objectivism of the historical method in favour of the total engagement of faith. A few years earlier he was interpreting Abraham as the knight of faith, the man who dared to go forward without any guarantees. Everyone seemed to think that the movement of faith was easily performed and, when performed, left behind as other objects were pursued. On the contrary, to believe God's promise that he should be the father of many nations through Isaac while the bright death quivered at the victim's throat, this was the highest passion in mankind, hardly attainable, never to be surpassed.

Kierkegaard stands at the opposite pole from the Ritschl-Harnack historical method. His solution to the problem was not one with which Barth at least could remain permanently satisfied. It was one, however, which provided him with the conviction and the courage to break decisively from his teachers. 'There is a river in the Bible that carries us away, once we have entrusted our destiny to it — away from ourselves to the sea. The Holy Scriptures will interpret themselves in spite of all our human limitations. We need only dare to follow this drive, this spirit, this river, to grow out beyond ourselves toward the highest answer. This daring is faith; and we read the Bible rightly, not when we do so with false modesty, restraint, and attempted sobriety, for these are passive qualities, but when we read it in faith' (p. 34). Such a statement would have been to Ritschl anathema, to Harnack nonsense.

It would appear to have been Thurneysen who introduced Barth to the works of Dostoevsky, those novels peopled by few conventional "saints" but by many unconventional sinners. Here the drunkard and the murderer, the prostitute and the epileptic, the gambler and the lecher, the leader of student violence and the atheist, live out their sordid, or their febrile, or their empty, days. And yet, incredible to relate, the general atmosphere of the novels is one of hope, sometimes quiet hope, sometimes joyful, sometimes incredulous, but hope. There might be written over them the wonderful and unforgettable inscription that stands in the chapel of the epileptic colony at Bethel-bei-Bielefeld: 'When the Lord turned again the captivity of Sion: then were we like unto them that dream. Then was our mouth filled with laughter: and our tongue with joy' (Psalm 126.1-2).

Into God's world, Barth had said in his lecture, 'the publicans and harlots will go before your impeccably elegant and righteous folk of good society' (p. 40). So it is in Dostoevsky. He has a high respect for morality, even respectability, and a corresponding disapproval of the immoral and the perverted. But he believes that it is through the forgiveness of sins that life everlasting is attained. Not only can there be the hope of renewed life for the murderer and the prostitute, prefigured in their reading together St John's account of the raising of Lazarus, but even the girl's father, the most irresponsible and depraved creature in *Crime and Punishment*, a drunkard who was to blame for his daughter's way of life, proclaims what is, on his lips and in the circumstances, a blasphemous caricature but, considered absolutely, is the pure gold of the Gospel. 'Why am I to be pitied, you say? Yes! There's nothing to pity me for! I ought to be crucified, crucified on a cross, not pitied! Crucify me, oh judge, crucify me but pity me! And then I will go of myself to be crucified, for it's not merrymaking I seek but tears and tribulation! . . . Do you suppose, you that sell, that this pint of yours has been sweet to me? It was tribulation I sought at the bottom of it, tears and tribulation, and have found it, and I have tasted it; but He will pity us Who has had pity on all men, Who has understood all men and all things. He is the One. He too is the judge. He will come in that day and He will ask: "Where is the daughter who gave herself for her cross, consumptive step-mother and for the little children of another? Where is the daughter who had pity upon the filthy drunkard, her earthly father, undismayed by his beastliness?" And He will say, "Come to Me! I have already forgiven thee once . . . . I have forgiven thee once . . . . Thy sins which are many are forgiven thee, for thou hast loved much . . . . " And He will forgive my Sonia, He will forgive, I know it . . . . I felt it in my heart when I was with her just now! And He will judge and will forgive all, the good and the evil, the wise and the meek . . . . And when He has done with all of them, then He will summon us. "You too come forth," He will say. "Come forth, ye drunkards, come forth, ye weak ones, come forth, ye children of shame!" And we shall all come forth, without shame and shall stand before Him. And He will say unto us: "Ye are swine, made in the Image of the Beast and with his mark; but come ye also!" And the wise ones and those of understanding will say: "Oh Lord, why dost Thou receive these men?" And He will say: "This is why I receive them, oh ye wise, this is why I receive them, oh ye of understanding, that not one of them believed himself to be worthy of this." And He will hold out His hands to us and we shall fall down before Him . . . and we shall weep . . . and we shall understand all things!' A better commentary on Luther's doctrine of justification by faith alone could not be imagined.

From Kierkegaard they learned how they should read the Bible; Dostoevsky provided a commentary on what they read. Their reading was 'a bit different' from that of their teachers because they not only rejected impartiality and unashamedly took sides, but because they attempted to disregard the differences of historical circumstances between themselves and the Bible and to treat this book as contemporary with themselves in Switzerland at a time when Dostoevsky's veiled prophecies on the future of Europe were beginning to be fulfilled in the madness of the nations and the suffering of mankind. There was no longer a difficulty in making the Bible relevant. It was already relevant, all too relevant; and its relevance could only be missed if it was, by the historical method, put in its place as a set of ancient documents.

It was at this point that Barth's theological genius asserted itself. To enter into the new world of the Bible and to purvey what was learned to the inhabitants of Safenwil and Leutwil in sermons and occasional lectures was a wonderful thing, but how could it hold its own against the general teaching of the Church, or the formidable scholarship of a Harnack or a Wernle? Indeed, there was the peril that they would end by becoming mere spir-

itual enthusiasts, rebels and iconoclasts whose inspiration would
serve them for a term, but who would then live only on their
hatred of the establishment. That Barth was early aware of the
danger appears from the letter of June 26, 1916: 'Our reflections of two weeks ago about renewed philosophical and theological studies stays with me and becomes ever more important
when considered from all aspects. The monologue with myself
and the little bit of dialogue with the congregation that I happen
to have, and also our common discussions — profitable as they
are — do not satisfy me in the long run. The area must be
widened and deepened from which I draw resources for inner
concentration and strengthening and upon which I would gladly
rely in working and speaking; otherwise I get no further than
wishing and am in danger of coming to a deadlock. It will not
do any longer that my sharpest and most basic thinking has to
do with what I want to *say*; otherwise one day there will be
nothing or next to nothing more to say. I think of myself as
one who lives on his private income, which is nothing. Further,
I say to myself that such a daring position as we so greatly desire to establish must have a solid foundation simply for the
sake of order, and that is not to be achieved by an occasional
bit of metaphysical construction sandwiched between administra-
tion and teaching. Finally, the matter itself presses urgently for
a more comprehensive treatment than is possible for a thirty-
year-old pastor in his practical sphere of activity. So, on with
the battle!' (*Rev. Theol.* p. 37).

But this is, in fact, a danger which has already been met,
for by now, it seems, Barth is engaged in the serious study of
St Paul's epistle to the Romans. At the end of July he writes:
'Discovery of a gold mine: J. T. Beck!! As a biblical expositor
he simply towers far above the rest of the company, also above
Schlatter .... I came on the track of him through my work on
Romans and will make use of him there along with the other
commentators from Calvin to Tholuck and as far as Kutter's
Righteousness, a whole cloud of witnesses!' (*Rev. Theol.* p. 38).
By September 1 he is 'wrestling with the granite block of 3.20ff.'
(p. 38), and has nearly finished the whole chapter by October
23. A year was to pass, however, before he had finished chapter

5. But it has now become his foremost occupation, even if there breaks in the parish a storm over the women's trade union in the knitting mill. In September 1917, in the midst of this local industrial struggle, he can live 'the whole week in strictest seclusion in his study and under the apple tree' (p. 43). It is clear also that the commentary is not being written for the private edification of himself and Thurneysen. It has been accepted for publication and the publishers want the manuscript by September 1, 1918, so that the book can catch the Christmas market. Although in March he had only arrived at 9,13, it would seem that he was able to deliver the manuscript more or less on time. for on the day the Armistice was signed he wrote that he was busy reading the proofs. Early in 1919 it was published after the long disappointments and frustrations which Barth hints at in his foreword to the 1963 reprinting of this first edition: 'The manuscript of this book originated in the years 1916-1918, that is, during the second half of the Great War. Three well known Swiss publishers — quite understandably, considering the times — refused it. There were then no Swiss national "grants" for such purposes; and if there had been, this undertaking by the minister of Safenwil would have found it difficult to get one. It was the Bern publisher G. A. Bäschlin who was at last willing to take on the risk and he did so because my friend, the Zürich merchant, Rudolf Pestalozzi, came to the rescue with most liberal financial support. It was out of the question to print more than a thousand copies. Just when the Swiss market seemed to be exhausted after the sale of three hundred copies, the book was "discovered" by Georg Merz, at the time a minister in München, and it was then taken over by the publishing firm of Christian Kaiser, under whose aegis the other seven hundred copies found in less than no time their German purchasers and readers'.

The Epistle to the Romans

1

BARTH'S COMMENTARY IS FAMILIAR TO THE ENGLISH-SPEAKING world through the translation by Sir Edwyn Hoskyns. But this was made from the revised edition, a vastly different book from the original of 1919. Almost their only likeness lies in the division into sections, though even here most of the titles of chapters and sections have been changed. It is by reading the titles that we can best gain an impression of the character of the commentary, its originality and force, its blend of the antique (which Emil Brunner noted) with modernity.

Chapter 1.   *Introduction*.
                        The Author to his Readers (1-7).
                        Personal Matters (8-15).
                        The Theme (16-17).
                 The Night
                        The Decline (18-21).
                        The Collapse (22-32).
Chapter 2.   *The Righteousness of Men*
                        God's Criterion (1-13).
                        Revaluation of all Values (14-29).
Chapter 3.   *The Righteousness of God*
                        Faithfulness (1-20).
                        Revelation (21-26).
                        Questions Answered (27-31).
Chapter 4.   *The Voice of the Bible*
                        God and the Hero (1-8).
                        Faith and Religion (9-12).
                        Righteousness and Morality (13-22).
                        History (23-25).
Chapter 5.   *The Day*
                        The New Situation (1-11).
                        The Victory of Life (12-21).
Chapter 6.   *Grace*
                        Good Friday (1-14).
                        Easter (15-23).

30

5. But it has now become his foremost occupation, even if there breaks in the parish a storm over the women's trade union in the knitting mill. In September 1917, in the midst of this local industrial struggle, he can live 'the whole week in strictest seclusion in his study and under the apple tree' (p. 43). It is clear also that the commentary is not being written for the private edification of himself and Thurneysen. It has been accepted for publication and the publishers want the manuscript by September 1, 1918, so that the book can catch the Christmas market. Although in March he had only arrived at 9,13, it would seem that he was able to deliver the manuscript more or less on time. for on the day the Armistice was signed he wrote that he was busy reading the proofs. Early in 1919 it was published after the long disappointments and frustrations which Barth hints at in his foreword to the 1963 reprinting of this first edition: 'The manuscript of this book originated in the years 1916-1918, that is, during the second half of the Great War. Three well known Swiss publishers — quite understandably, considering the times — refused it. There were then no Swiss national "grants" for such purposes; and if there had been, this undertaking by the minister of Safenwil would have found it difficult to get one. It was the Bern publisher G. A. Bäschlin who was at last willing to take on the risk and he did so because my friend, the Zürich merchant, Rudolf Pestalozzi, came to the rescue with most liberal financial support. It was out of the question to print more than a thousand copies. Just when the Swiss market seemed to be exhausted after the sale of three hundred copies, the book was "discovered" by Georg Merz, at the time a minister in München, and it was then taken over by the publishing firm of Christian Kaiser, under whose aegis the other seven hundred copies found in less than no time their German purchasers and readers'.

The Epistle to the Romans

1

Barth's commentary is familiar to the English-speaking world through the translation by Sir Edwyn Hoskyns. But this was made from the revised edition, a vastly different book from the original of 1919. Almost their only likeness lies in the division into sections, though even here most of the titles of chapters and sections have been changed. It is by reading the titles that we can best gain an impression of the character of the commentary, its originality and force, its blend of the antique (which Emil Brunner noted) with modernity.

Here was no commentary repeating or even explicating what Paul had once said to the Roman Christians, but one that designed to translate Paul's thoughts into such a form and language as would uncover their immediate relevance in the world of 1919. That as the letter had once spoken directly to the first century, so it should speak its same message directly to the twentieth. It is true that this intention is vain without the previous understanding of what Paul was saying to his contemporaries. But such a previous understanding is only the first step in the process of apprehending and embracing the meaning of Scripture. Thus one section (2.14-29) bears as its title the well-known tag from Nietzsche, "Revaluation of all Values". Something is being said to the Europe which not long since has heard the revolutionary demand for the abolition of all religion. It could not have been expressed in this way fifty years before. But it is the post-Nietzschean way of saying 'that God does *not* acknowledge man's righteousness, but has, along with unrighteousness, "shut it up under unbelief" (11.32) in order to let *his* righteousness appear' (p. 41). Barth is aware of the irremovable necessity for faithful exegesis, with its attendant disciplines of history in various forms and of literary criticism. 'But far more important than this truth is the other, that as Prophet and Apostle of the kingdom of God he speaks to all men of every age' (p. V).

Barth stands, then, in that line of men to whom the message of Romans has been a word creative of liberty. In the first century Paul had cut the Gospel of Jesus Christ free from the bondage of Judaism by binding Judaism inescapably to Jesus Christ. In the fifth century Augustine, himself first liberated by Romans 13.11-16, applied the Pauline doctrine to the neo-Judaism of Pelagius. Eleven hundred years later the Reformation turned the same doctrine against the neo-Judaism of the late medieval Church. At that time many commentaries on Romans were published. One, however, lay unprinted and in comparative obscurity. From Easter 1515 until September 1516 Luther lectured on Romans in Wittenberg. His lectures were virtually lost until they were at last published in 1908. It would not be over-romantic to see in the fate of these lectures a symbol of the substance of the Epistle itself, shining in such brilliant light in the Reformation, but dimmed and obscured thereafter for three centuries.

Barth's *Epistle to the Romans* takes up again the task of Augustine and the Reformers. But now the doctrine is directed against the neo-Judaism of religion itself, specifically of Protestantism under the sway of Schleiermacher and Ritschl, but this as representing religion itself, any endeavour whatsoever of man to make his knowledge or experience of God the basis of the knowledge or experience of God. The first edition, however, is a remarkably positive book, an affirmation of the deity and

sovereignty of God, of his faithfulness, of his salvation in Jesus
Christ. The negations proceed when the life and theology of the
Church are measured against these affirmations. The attacks on
religion and culture are made in the interests of revelation and
faith. The pious and the righteous are disestablished, morality
and religion relativized; but this is because men are redeemed
by the faithfulness of God in the Christ. The whole concept of
history associated with the "historical method" comes under
assault; but this is because there is a proper, a true, history which
is the activity of God in the Christ and which is covered over
when the "historical method" reigns in New Testament studies.

Most of the forty-two sections into which the work is divided are cast in the same form. They begin with a general introduction preparing the way for the exposition. The exposition
itself is sometimes preceded by the relevant text of the epistle,
Barth's own rendering from the Nestlé text; but sometimes the
text is interwoven with the exposition, sometimes it is placed
even at the end. In style the first edition will come as a surprise
to those who know only the English translation of the second
edition. H. R. Mackintosh mentions an un-named "admirer"
who spoke of Barth striding 'along clad in a scientific terminology which is hard, intricate, and every way exacting' (*Types of
Modern Theology*, p. 263). But in the first edition the language
is generally clear, easily understood; the sentences not often long,
the vocabulary not unusual, the imagery restrained. Why, then,
did there arise such criticism of its difficulty? No doubt from two
causes: its ideas ran counter to the thought of the period; and
they were cast in a form remote from what the Pauline text
led the reader to expect. Every word in a sentence might be
simple, its grammatical structure straightforward, but the surprising juxtaposition of the words, the concentration of the
thought, with perhaps a certain over-writing, often leaves the
reader at the last unenlightened, even if considerably excited.

A passage where clarity of language and obscurity of concept walk hand in hand is the first paragraph of the section 'God
and the Hero' with which Chapter 4 opens: 'The meaning of
history is God's meaning. That is now obvious. And by this is
indicated where the ways of the past come from and where the

ways of the future are leading. The present time, the dawning end of all times, opens up for us now a view into the eternal in past and future. The revelation in the Christ is certainly not an 'historical' event, but the irruption of the power which was present and will be present, the uncovering of the ever active, the essential, the reality in the vast strata of the ages. Because God's work in the Christ comes forth to view, it is revealed also as the hidden unity of the whole of history. The light of God's day throws its beams both forwards and backwards. Since the divine will with mankind has become clear in the Christ at one point of time, the whole of time, from its beginning to its furthest future, can be no longer considered as a confused conglomeration of innumerable individuals closed within themselves as "window-less monads", who have innumerable and different relationships to God. The divine will in history is not an area of larger and smaller ruins, static as all ruins, but a rolling sphere (Ezekiel 1.15f.), mobile, always equal to itself, whole and complete in itself at each point of time. And the historical individuals form a solidarity, one family in one and the same house, certainly differentiated and graded, always according to their particular relationship to the great course of prophecy, accomplishing, and fulfilment, as fore-runners, contemporaries, and successors of the Messiah, but (which is more important than the difference!) united by what they have in common, the Kingdom of God come nigh in the Messiah. In the knowledge of the immediacy of the Christ to God it becomes clear that each epoch has its own particular immediacy to God' (p. 75).

In language and syntax this passage certainly cannot be justly called difficult. There are few places in the *Church Dogmatics* compared with which it would not shine as simplicity. And yet if we try to analyze it, how obscure so much of it becomes. Few, however, of those who read it when it first appeared attempted a cool analysis. The author's general intention was plain, to let the voice of the Bible, as concentrated in Romans, be heard by the men of his generation. Here was no persuasive reason, no fair presentation of both sides of the question, no scholarly reserve. All was affirmation or negation, unmistakable, firm, vigorous. What is more, affirmation and negation in cosmic dimensions; the talk is of the Kingdom of God and the World, of the old and the new Aeons, of Origins and of Death, and of the Victory of Life, of the Spirit, of the Christ. Many of its readers were seized by the conviction that here was the word from heaven for which they too had been waiting. The nine-teenth century, personified theologically by Schleiermacher and Ritschl, had burnt out in the Great War. If culture and piety could not prevent the War, how could they rebuild Europe after the War? Here now was a voice saying with assurance and all the power of theological genius what many a Bible reader had felt in his heart but had not been able to formulate, or had not dared say, lacking the necessary self-confidence in the face of the common opinion of the learned. And for the ordinary minister the voice had a further recommendation, that it did not proceed from a professorial study or lecture room but from the study in a manse, the pulpit in a village church. Barth's experi-ences and problems were doubtless the same as theirs. He had justification and right to call to them to be converted to the Bible, to read the Bible a bit differently. It is not hard to see how and why the book made such zealous disciples — though whether Barth made more disciples in these years for himself or for Kierkegaard is perhaps another question.

If the book won zealous disciples, it made no less inexo-rable enemies. The "great blow against the theologians" had been struck. The theologians now began to single themselves out as friends or foes, to applaud or to retaliate. Some of the decisions taken were surprising. Who would have guessed that Barth would be rejected by Schlatter, that godly man concerned that the message of the New Testament should come to light again? It was the second edition of *The Epistle to the Romans* that Schlatter reviewed, but his criticisms are valid of the first. He, the first of the "evangelicals" to refuse Barth, shows him-self firmly entrenched in the "historical method" after all: 'In the exposition of chapters one and two we hear nothing of the Greek religion and its devastating effects, of the synagogue and its religious failure, of the law, which at that time ordered by its very concrete norms the conduct of all who looked to God. You, the reader, are the Greek; you are also the Jew; and your sole concern must be that the word of Paul reaches you and shows you the divine wrath, which sinks you with all your piety into nothingness' (*Dialectic Theology*, pp. 122-3). Later he repeats this complaint, but gives another view of the book's character: 'Since the exegete does not wish to say anything to us about the history of Roman Christendom, of Israel, of Paul and Jesus, what is he then going to talk to us about? He becomes the exegete of his own life and the interpreter of his own heart' (p. 122).

The best review, both for good and ill, came from Adolf Jülicher, and paid the book the compliment not only of five columns in *Die Christliche Welt* but of a good piece of writing. Jülicher begins with sarcastic comments on 'that presumptuous Foreword', in which the author 'indicates that he has now understood the Apostle Paul . . . while the critical historical method of biblical research teaches us to understand him only provisionally as a child of his time speaking to his contemporaries . . . . If Barth should deceive himself in the cheerful hope for a joint new research and quest for the biblical message, then this book has time to — wait; the Letter to the Romans itself is still waiting' (*Dialectic Theology*, p. 72). After this piece of pleasantry, Jülicher goes on with a review which is remarkable for its awareness of the danger in the attack on the "historical" position, for its unconsciousness that any other position is feasible, and for its generous recognition of Barth's abilities: 'The author has at his disposal superb gifts for attaining [his] goal. . . . He knows how to speak penetratingly, at times charmingly, and always with colourful vividness' (p. 72). Even he will go so far as to say: 'The Barthian Paulinism is a landmark on the road of church history' (p. 81). On the other hand, he does not conceal his pain at Barth's attempts at textual criticism: 'He makes his decisions in such cases with remarkable haste' (p. 75). And he spoke truly and authoritatively when he summed it up: 'These scholarly notes — they are not at all numerous — would all have been better left out, because they clash with the style of this work and offer nothing new. It would have been better for Barth to have avoided giving the impression that he had independent ability to deal with the manuscript transmission of Ro-

mans and its families of texts. Unfortunately, he relied heavily
on Zahn. Where he differed — I mean, in matters of text-critical
and exegetical difficulty — he chose poorly' (p. 75).

But when the review came on to the substance of Romans
and the principles of interpretation, the positions are reversed.
Jülicher was a better historian than theologian and therefore
tended to express himself by way of historical parallels. Barth,
he says, passes through the historical to the Spirit — 'This is
exactly the standpoint of Origen' (p. 78). He then compares him
with Marcion. By seeing Barth in relation to the greatest early
representative of the "spiritual" method of interpretation and to
the heretic who had 'the same one-sided dualistic approach of
enmity to all that comes from the world, culture, or tradition'
(p. 78), Jülicher is in effect counter-attacking from the two central positions of nineteenth century Protestantism against which
The Epistle to the Romans was directed, the historical method
of Biblical interpretation and the understanding of a culture as
a revelation from God.

Jülicher's review is of the highest importance, for it is an
essential product of the enemy which Barth had attacked. It
deals with the heart of the matter. And so firmly entrenched is
it that it cannot conceive of the validity of any alternative.
Throughout, an admiration for Barth's intellectual gifts struggles
with an amazed sorrow at his spiritual madness and arrogance.
For Jülicher it is unthinkable that any sane person, let alone a
scholar, could occupy Barth's position.

Barth took, or pretended to take, the review with cheerful
indifference. He wrote to Thurneysen on July 14, 1920: 'There!
Yesterday afternoon Jülicher's long-heralded 42-centimeter
shell landed here . . . . Help me to take the measurements of
the shell-hole and to dig out whatever rubble there is. But it is
not really bad, more a gentle evening rain that moistens everything than a fearful thunderstorm' (*Rev. Theol.* p. 52). But the
gentle rain had penetrated deep into the soil. Even in this letter
Barth shows his uneasiness under Jülicher's learned criticisms:
'And in the presence of these scholars who know twenty-five
times as much as we do we shall in the future lift our hats more
respectfully, even though it seems to us quite idolatrous' (pp. 52-3).

Perhaps what had fallen had not been rain after all but the 42-centimeter shell, which had helped to demolish the commentary.

2.

By now the new publishers, Christian Kaiser Verlag, were planning a second edition, incorporating, it would seem, some corrections by the author. But these plans were upset when, three months after Jülicher's review, Barth spent a few days in the company of Friedrich Gogarten. Gogarten was at this time minister of Stelzendorf in Thüringia. The most ruthless of theologians, anything savouring of subjectivity was the special object of his hatred, and he rode out to destroy Schleiermacher, pietism, and "Christian" culture. Gogarten was in truth what Barth was commonly and unjustly supposed to be, a fierce and stern foe, capable of uttering only the negative.

In 1920 he published a short essay under the title *Zwischen den Zeiten* — literally, 'Between the times'. Direct, without adornment, brutally clear, *Zwischen den Zeiten* tore the "new" theology asunder from liberal Protestantism: 'It is the destiny of our generation to stand between the times.... So we stand in the middle — in an empty space. We belong neither to the one nor to the other. Not to the one which precedes us, which would like to make us its disciples and the heirs of its thoughts and convictions. We cannot follow them. We never could. When we did, it was only to see how they worked — but never to have a model or example for our own actions.... Your concepts were strange to us, always strange' (*Dialectic Theology*, p. 277). The death of the old "refined, intelligent culture", as foretold in Spengler's *Decline of the West*, is welcomed with jubilation. For through it God has been lost, and we have now realized the fact and accepted it. All we can do at present is to 'know more and more distinctly what he is not, what he cannot be' (p. 279). What can we do, we who stand in a different realm from you and no longer hope for progress? We do not know. 'The only practical suggestion we can make is the following.... to recognize with dismay ... that clever suggestions can no longer help in the situation in which we all find ourselves' (p.

281). And accordingly the essay ends: 'We should guard ourselves in this hour from nothing so much as from considering what we should do now. We stand, not before our own wisdom, but before God. This hour is not our hour. *We* have no time now. *We* stand *zwischen den Zeiten*' (p. 282).

Off wrote Barth to Thurneysen in June: 'Have you read Gogarten's *Zwischen den Zeiten* in the *Christliche Welt*? I sent him a greeting at once and called upon him to cry aloud. This is good' (*Rev. Theol.* p. 52).

The greeting must have led to a correspondence and an invitation, for on October 27 Barth writes that Gogarten has been staying at Safenwil. He goes on: 'Here is a dreadnought on our side and against our opponents. Who knows, perhaps one day yet he will teach us something . . . . I have great expectations concerning him . . . . perhaps one day he will make some kind of an enormous breach in the theological wall' (p. 53).

Out of Gogarten's visit came directly the second edition of *The Epistle to the Romans*. To describe the new book as the result of his influence on Barth would be going too far. We merely record the fact that immediately upon the visit and its many long talks Barth suddenly determined that the commentary could not be republished in its present form and at the same time saw just how it should be revised: 'And now a strange and decisive bit of news: when Gogarten, with whom I had so many good conversations by day and night, was gone, suddenly the *Letter to the Romans* began to shed its skin; that is, I received the enlightenment that, as it now stands, it is simply impossible that it should be reprinted; rather it must be reformed root and branch' (*Rev. Theol.* p. 53). Indeed, he had already set to work, for he was able to enclose in this letter several pages for Thurneysen's judgment, and had sent a telegram to the publishers announcing his new intention. The message was not well received. The remaining copies of the first edition were now selling so fast that they hoped to get a reprint on the market before Christmas and dispose of it before a revised edition was printed. Throughout the winter of 1920 and the spring and summer of 1921 he was toiling at the work of revision, wishing that he had a curate to take some of the parish work off his hands. 'During the past years,' he said in the Preface to the second edition, the people of Safenwil 'have had to put up with a pastor who lived in his study' (p. 15). And to Thurneysen in August: 'I amble like a drunk man back and forth between writing desk, dining table, and bed, travelling each kilometer with my eye already on the next one' (p. 59).

By September he was writing his Preface, and the second edition appeared in the early part of 1922. A third edition followed in July of this year, a fourth in February 1924, a fifth in February 1926, and the sixth and last in Advent 1928. The preface to each successive edition is a little piece of intellectual autobiography. That to the second edition will serve to explain the book itself to us. It bears an enigmatic prefix, the Greek of Galatians 1.17: 'Neither went I up to Jerusalem . . . but I went away into Arabia.' Here, Barth tells us, is a completely new book; practically nothing remains unaltered from the first edition. Since I finished the first edition I have engaged in a renewed study of Paul himself, and also of Overbeck, Plato and Kant, Kierkegaard and Dostoevsky. The results of these studies appear plainly in the new edition. Yet it should not be supposed that this second edition is different from the first in its essence or in its basic views. The difference lies in their form. But they have it in common that they are both unashamedly theological commentaries. Jülicher criticised the first edition for being theological. But I have never claimed to be anything but a theologian. If I am not mistaken, we theologians serve laymen best when we do our job as honest theologians and are not trying to meet them on their own ground. Other critics were put out because I did not speak in a simple manner. But the understanding of God in the Bible is not simple. Perhaps in thirty years time we may be able to speak simply; at present let us be content only with speaking the truth; in every respect human life is difficult; pseudo-simplicity will help no one. Yet others have accused me of rejecting Biblical criticism. This is based on a misunderstanding. When, in the first edition, I protested against certain modern commentaries, I was referring not only to liberals but also to conservatives. My objection is to the type of commentary that reconstructs the text, translates the Greek words and phrases by their vernacular equivalents, and adds philological, archaeological, and historical annotations. It stops short of the actual understanding and interpretation of the document . . . . For example, compare Jülicher with Calvin. Jülicher never comes to grips with Paul's thought, but treats it merely as ancient history; when he has finished, the document is still no nearer intelligibility. But Calvin — 'how energetically Calvin, having established what stands in the text, sets himself to re-think the whole material and to wrestle with it, till the walls which separate the sixteenth century from the first become transparent! Paul speaks, and the man of the sixteenth century hears' (p. 7). I am far from wishing an abolition of Biblical criticism. On the contrary, the critic must become more critical, in order that he may be confronted simply by the message of the document, and that the Word may be laid bare in the words. This is no academic question; it concerns the very life of the Church. The students who are being trained in the "critical" study of the Bible are those who will have to preach. Their training does not fit them for the understanding of the Bible that preaching demands. 'I myself know what it means year in year out to mount the steps of the pulpit, conscious of the responsibility to understand and to interpret, and longing to fulfil it; and yet, utterly incapable, because at the University I had never been brought beyond that well-known 'Awe in the presence of history' which means in the end no more than that all hope of engaging in the dignity of understanding and interpretation has been surrendered' (p. 9). I have been accused, too, of reading my own theology into the epistle. But all I have done is to make the assumption that in Romans Paul was writing about Jesus Christ and not about someone else, and I interpret him on that assumption. How can this be regarded as reading something into the epistle? Wernle has accused me of Biblicism, and is surprised I should take certain aspects of Paul's teaching seriously: 'the Pauline "depreciation" of the earthly life of Jesus — Christ the Son of God — Redemption by the blood of Christ — Adam and Christ — Paul's use of the Old Testament — his so-called Baptismal-Sacramentalism — The Double Predestination — his attitude to secular authority' (p. 12). But all

these occur in the epistle and have to be understood and interpreted.

Barth, then, intends his commentary to be theological. *The
Epistle to the Romans* is theological in that it engages with Paul's
doctrines as a living issue and re-states them in the modern
author's own manner. If there is something here of Calvin, there
is much of Kierkegaard. The Bible is like a love-letter, he says
in *The Mirror of the Word*, and should be read in the same way.
If the letter is written in a foreign language, the lover will need
to decipher it with the aid of a dictionary, but he will regard the
toil of translation as an irritating delay to the reading of the
letter, a necessary evil, and he will certainly not imagine that
he is reading the letter while he is still translating it. Therefore,
'If thou art a learned man, then take care lest with all thy erudite reading (which is not reading God's Word) thou forgettest
perchance to read God's Word' (pp. 53-4). Erudite reading is all
too easily a way of defending oneself against God's Word: 'For
take the Holy Scriptures — shut thy door; but take also ten dic-
tionaries, twenty commentaries, and then thou canst read it just
as tranquilly and unembarrassed as thou dost read a newspaper
column' (p. 56). Genuine reading of the Scriptures means reading it as a message personal to oneself and thereupon putting
into effect whatever that message enjoins. In this sermon, published in 1851, before Ritschl had even become a professor,
Kierkegaard attacked the historical method which he was to
represent: 'The greater part regard God's Word as an antiquated
document of olden time which one puts aside, and a smaller
part regards God's Word as an exceedingly notable document of
olden time upon which one expends an astonishing amount of
diligence and acumen, &c . . . beholding the mirror' (p. 58).

The lesson was plain, even if Kierkegaard taught it in so
one-sided a fashion as almost to defeat his purpose. Barth heeded
the lesson and disregarded its manner. He was too good a scholar
to despise scholarship, and it may well be that the learned little
notes that offended Jülicher were meant to re-assure critics that
he was no ignorant Biblicist, but gave learning its due place. The
main thing, however, was that the lesson was assimilated. Romans
was treated as a living voice which spoke to the twentieth cen-

tury no less clearly and loudly than to the first or the sixteenth.

Romans is a theological letter. It proclaims God's eternal purpose in Jesus Christ, and therefore his judgment on all men and his gracious reconciliation with men. The whole history of mankind is seen only in its relationship to God. The life of individual men and of groups is not given an independent validity but placed in relationship to God. This viewpoint is not anthropological or cosmological but theological. Barth's commentary strives to accord with this. He therefore insists with all his powers on the independent reality of God. So long as God is confused with man, God's spirit with man's spirit, God's revelation with man's religion, it is impossible to understand Romans, where God is a separate being from man. Hence Barth's less than comely synonym for God, "the Wholly Other"; hence such dicta as 'The Gospel proclaims a God utterly distinct from men'; hence also the nexus of mathematical images that we shall soon examine. Barth himself states this in the Preface as the heart of the matter for him: 'If I have a system, it is limited to a recognition of what Kierkegaard called the "infinite qualitative distinction" between time and eternity, and to my regarding this as possessing negative as well as positive significance: "God is in heaven, and thou art on earth." The relation between such a God and such a man, and the relation between such a man and such a God, is for me the theme of the Bible and the essence of philosophy' (p. 10). But this carries no less surely the positive significance that Jesus Christ, Son of God and Son of Man, is the point of intersection where heaven meets earth, where God reveals himself to man as Reconciler and Lord.

The substance of *The Epistle to the Romans* is theological. But its language is not highly technical: 'God', 'grace', 'faith', 'sin', 'judgment', 'justification', 'resurrection', and the like meet us at every turn, but there is little in the way of the sophisticated terminology that is to be found in the *Church Dogmatics*. Although this second edition is vastly more difficult to understand than the first, the cause still lies rather in the formulation of the concepts than in the language. Now, however, the directness of 1919 has given place to a magnificence and sublimity that takes the reader by storm.

A large part of the magnificence is due to the abundance of imagery. In this the *Epistle to the Romans* is, I think, unique among Barth's books; certainly in neither the first edition nor in the *Church Dogmatics* is such a fire-work display laid on. Here the numerous and inter-related images form an integral and essential part of the commentary.

There are first the mathematical images, generally based on an elementary mathematics that any boy in the middle school would know. From geometry we have the intersection of planes: 'In this name [Jesus Christ] two worlds meet and go apart, two planes intersect, the one known and the other unknown' (p. 29). Or, conveying almost the same idea, the tangent which touches a circle without, of course, touching it. The resurrection of Jesus Christ is such a paradox, historical event and non-historical event. The tangent occurs rarely, however, as does the modest piece of algebra that the minus sign before the bracket reverses the plus and minus signs within the brackets. It is the image of a plane and the intersection of planes that runs through the book, changing as it goes into other images. The plane itself, a straight line, becomes a signpost pointing to a certain place where it itself is not, but which the traveller must journey to. (Related to this is Barth's understanding of the crucifixion in the Isenheim Altarpiece by Grünewald, where John the Baptist's pointing finger is like a signpost to the Lamb of God. We are here in the realm of signs and sacraments and testimony. This aspect of the painting and its imagery impressed itself profoundly on the minds of Barth and his associates in the nineteen-twenties, and occurs in different contexts, as when his brother, Peter Barth, says that 'The Institutio is like Calvin's fore-finger, pointing us to the Scriptures'). But the plane is then transformed into the line which marks a frontier between two countries, in this case between heaven and earth. (The tangent also touches the circle as its frontier). We remain on this side of the frontier ('The whole burden of sin and the whole curse of death still press heavily upon us', p. 38), but we gaze across the frontier to the new land, and become watchmen — the image is at once changed — watching 'for the dawning of the day' (p. 38). A frontier, however, also represents a barrier which may not be passed: 'Must it be assumed that we all stand before the barrier, and that, unless we are aware of our positions, we must remain barred up and our lives but vanity and darkness?' (p. 55). But behold! the plane, the frontier, the barrier, has, like some surrealist film, melted into prison bars, and we have the image of man's imprisonment. A few lines later and all the bars save one have disappeared, and man stands at the bar of God's judgment. And everywhere the plane is *die Todeslinie*, the line of death, now the boundary or prison which hems in man's life, now human life itself or religion, its manifestation. But from God's side *die Todeslinie* is its opposite, *die Lebenslinie*, the line of life.

The intersection of the two planes has its own history. The vertical and descending plane becomes a shell which bursts on the earth. This image is used to say that revelation (the intersection of the planes, the bursting of the shell) is not a permanent state. After the shell-burst all that is left is a burnt crater in the ground. Such a crater is the Church: 'the activity of the community is related to the Gospel only in so far as it is no more than a crater formed by the explosion of a shell and seeks to be no more than a void in which the Gospel reveals itself' (p. 36). Such a crater is also the law, but here at once it becomes a different sort of hole in the ground, a hole that is also a straight line, a dry canal once filled with the living water of faith. For this concept that revelation is an event and not a state but that certain states still bear marks that they have been the means of revelation Barth uses also the image of the stamped impress, which positively is a genuine representation of the seal but negatively is precisely its opposite.

It is noteworthy that few of the images are organic, not many human (e.g. the watchman, the soldier, the rebel) but most either technological, inanimate, or taken from the realm of pure thought, i.e. mathematical. The arts make a brief appearance or two in the costume of music. But the aesthetic and organic images are strangely trite. The Gospel is "the seed of eternity" and the "fruit of time" (p. 28). 'One drop of eternity is of greater weight than a vast ocean of finite things' (p. 77). 'The discord of human defiance is penetrated by the undertones of the divine melody "Nevertheless" ' (p. 95). There is an interesting exception, however, in the image of mist, referred usually to the effect of religion on men: 'Once the eye . . . has been blinded, there arises in the midst, between here and there, between us and the "Wholly Other", a mist or concoction of religion in which, by a whole series of skilful assimilations and mixings more or less strongly flavoured with sexuality, sometimes the behaviour of men or of animals is exalted to be an experience of God, sometimes the Being and Existence of God is "enjoyed" as a human or animal experience' (pp. 49-50). The mist envelopes us, so that we cannot see clearly. It is 'a tiny mist between God and man' which soon becomes 'a veritable sea of clouds' (p. 52).

There is one more image to be mentioned, which is so central to Barth's thinking at this time that the whole movement was called after it: *The Theology of Crisis*. The Greek word *krisis* bore the meaning of separating out one thing from another, and hence of making a decision, or even of passing sentence in a law court. It does not occur in Romans, and indeed it is not a word much used by Paul, but is more associated with Johannine theology. Barth, however, used it frequently in his second edition, and, as his manner was, with an intricate and complex set of meanings. It was an admirable word for his purpose. It fitted the concept of the judgment of God that runs through Romans, with its attendant image of a court of law. It also carried undertones of the cognate word 'critical', perhaps with a backward look at Kant's two titles, *The Critique of Pure Reason* and *The Critique of Practical Reason*, but certainly with the reminder to the *critics* that *criticism* is not an ultimate but also stands under *criticism*. In German as in English 'crisis' has a wide range of reference. A crisis is a moment of danger in the affairs of a nation, a group, an individual. It is also a turning-point, as in some diseases. The Churches were in danger, their sickness had reached the decisive point of death or recovery. All these meanings lie within Barth's use of *krisis*.

A brief appendix to the first edition had indicated some of the books that Barth had drawn upon: 'among the books on Romans that I have used I should like . . . to mention the following as particularly valuable to me: the Commentary of Calvin

(1539), Bengel's N. T. Gnomon (1742), C. H. Rieger's Thoughts
on the N. T. (1828), the Commentaries and Expositions of F.
Godet (1881), J. T. Beck (1886), Schlatter (1887), Lietzmann
(1906) and T. Zahn (1910), Kutter's *Righteousness* (Rom. 1-8;
1905) and his articles on Romans in the *Kirchenfreund* of 1894,
an unpublished course of lectures by my father, and finally, for
the general orientation on Paul and the early church, F. Zündel's
Apostolic Age (1886) and Albert Schweitzer's *History of the
Study of Paul* (1911)' (p. 439). But, as we saw in Chapter One,
the point of view from which he interpreted Paul was not learned
from writers on Romans but from the Bible itself read over the
shoulders of Dostoevsky and Kierkegaard and the Christian
Socialists. These influencing spirits remain off-stage for most of
the time, and instead we hear a good deal from Goethe and
Schiller and the little-known poet Spitteler.

Now in the second edition, all this changes. The place of
Goethe, Schiller and Spitteler knows them no more. In their
stead stand Calvin and Luther, Dostoevsky and Blumhardt,
Kierkegaard, Nietzsche and Overbeck. It was Franz Overbeck
who most powerfully stimulated the minds of Barth and Thurneysen in these years. Overbeck had become Professor of Church
History at Basel as long ago as 1870. He had been the close
friend of Nietzsche and it was, indeed, he who had taken charge
of the philosopher and his affairs when Nietzsche became ir-
revocably insane some twenty years later. Yet it would be un-
just to class him merely as the friend of Nietzsche. He had his
own strong views on the meaning of Christianity and the evil
influence of theology on religion.

The first reference to him in the letters is Barth's report
in April 1920 that he has visited his widow, 'a lively, sensible
old lady' (*Rev. Theol.* p. 50). But he and Thurneysen had been
studying Overbeck to such good purpose that they had written a
book on him: *On the Inner Situation of Christianity* (reprinted
in *Theology and Church* under the title 'Unsettled Questions for
Theology Today'). What had the anti-theologian of Basel to
contribute to their theology? Precisely his sceptical view that
Christianity and history do not belong together, that when Christianity assumes an historical form it ceases to be Christian and

becomes demonic. And that this, far from being merely a potential threat, is what has in fact happened early in the course of Church history. His was a critique that both deposed the historical method from its sovereignty in New Testament study and also forbade the identification of Christianity with any culture, however exalted. Theology itself, far from being beautiful and joyous, is, he said, 'the Satan of religion' (*Theology and Church*, p. 69). Barth refused to take this as Overbeck's final word and pointed to passages in his writings where he speaks of the re-establishment of a theology which is willing to renounce 'all its pretensions, historical, scientific, and theological' (p. 72).

Led by Overbeck, Kierkegaard and Dostoevsky, and accompanied by Eduard Thurneysen, Barth had trodden the way to the desert in which *The Epistle to the Romans* was written and which he never afterwards left. 'We must urgently warn all those who desire positive results and directions that they should not rush too quickly towards the standpoint which Overbeck indicated, but did not himself employ. Still less should they suppose that the promised land will be reached tomorrow — perhaps even today! Our next task is to begin the desert wandering' (*Theology and Church*, p. 73).

CHAPTER THREE

Deflection to Dogmatics

EXTERNALLY THE ROAD LED INTO ANYTHING BUT A DESERT. BARTH was in the midst of revising *The Epistle to the Romans* when he was invited to fill the newly created chair of Reformed Theology in the Lutheran faculty at Göttingen. He was not, humanly speaking, wedded indissolubly to the parochial life. His first hope, indeed, had been for an academic career. After his two semesters at Marburg, he had stayed on there for a year (October 1908-1909). This was chiefly, as we have seen, to assist Martin Rade with the periodical *Die Christliche Welt*; but he hoped at the same time to write a thesis under Wilhelm Herrmann. No doubt success in this venture would have set his feet upon the lower rungs of the academic ladder. Unfortunately he discovered that the subject he had chosen had been used in another thesis, at Strasbourg, and his bid came to nothing. Thirteen years passed before he had another chance. It is understandable that when he is invited to Göttingen we find him saying, not without bitterness, that he had been 'chewing wearily for twelve years on the one half of the sour theological apple, in the pastoral office' (*Rev. Theol.* p. 58). When in 1925 Barth was offered the parish of Neumünster near Zürich, he remembered Safenwil, and refused: 'I am troubled by the memory of how greatly, how yet *more* greatly, I *failed* finally as a pastor of Safenwil, so very different, e.g., from you in Leutwil. The prospect of having to teach children again, of having to take hold of all kinds of practical problems . . . is really fearful to me' (*Rev. Theol.* p. 230).

It was therefore with little more than a conventional *nolo professorari* that he accepted the invitation and in the first week of October 1921 moved into the heart of alien Germany. The beginning of 1922 brought an honorary Doctorate of Theology from the University of Münster. Thus we now see the pastor of

Safenwil transformed at the touch of the wand into the Professor and Doctor at Göttingen.

The change was not easy. He had to work very hard to acquire proficiency in technical theology; he was in demand far and near as an occasional lecturer; the strain of work and worry told on his health; he and his colleagues grew out of sympathy with one another; he was trying to find a new way in theology; and he was living in post-war Germany with its bitter memories, cruel present and dangerous future.

It was going back to school again that proved so hard. He must as an undergraduate have possessed the basic skills of languages and historical knowledge. But the greatest peril to the minister who is also a part-time theologian is that he studies only what is immediately necessary. He may even become very learned, but it will be within strait limits. Barth must have read widely in preparation for his commentary on Romans. But it was eclectic reading; he read only those books that in one way or another would help him to understand Romans. He was in danger of becoming a despiser of history altogether, for he writes of 'how frightfully indifferent I have become about the purely historical questions' (*Rev. Theol.* p. 36). But now there was demanded of him, and he had acquiesced in the demand, that he should teach historical theology.

The groans sound and resound. If only he had spent more time at Safenwil on these things instead of on reading the newspaper! 'My thorn in the flesh, my dreadful theological ignorance, sharpened by my quite miserable memory' (*Rev. Theol.* p. 92). He complains of his 'weak Latin' (p. 137). 'I have to be under pressure to be adequately prepared' (p. 76). He lives from hand to mouth, sometimes writing far into the night lectures that he delivered at seven the next morning. He is not afraid of work; all he wants is 'time, time, time, to do everything *properly*, to read everything at *my own* tempo, to take it apart and put it together again' (p. 93). But alas! lack of time is a malady most incident to men. Barth achieved miracles of study within the next five years.

Through letters to Thurneysen we can trace his steps. His first two courses of lectures were on the Heidelberg Catechism and on Ephesians. Perhaps these subjects were chosen because he already had done some work on them: certainly he had preached a course at Safenwil on Ephesians in 1919. At any rate, by January 1922 he was occupied 'chiefly with the Reformation and everything connected with it' (p. 81). He has a lecture on Calvin in the following summer for which he is already preparing. Calvin, however, drove him back to the medieval schoolmen, while at the same time he was studying Luther and Zwingli. Unfortunately the haste in which he worked forced him into poor methods. He was for the moment collecting the 'essential ideas' of these authors together, 'leaving a proper study of the sources for a later and a better time' (p. 93). How he discovered that these really were their essential ideas we do not learn. The book on which he seems largely to have relied was Hagenbach's *History of Doctrines*. Despite its age (first edition 1840, last edition 1866) he preferred it to the more modern works by Loofs, Harnack, and Reinhold Seeberg on account of its numerous quotations from the sources. One great advantage that he possessed was that he inherited his father's theological library.

Quite quickly he determines his field of study. First, he chooses Calvin's theology and postpones his ethics to a later course. Next, having originally intended a concurrent course on Hebrews, he decides to drop this and concentrate on Calvin: 'Calvin and all that is involved with him alone claims me *wholly* . . . . to do justice to my professorship I must concentrate my attention primarily upon the history of dogma and let the New Testament alone for a while' (p. 96).

Whether, in spite of all his hard work and his enthusiasm, he succeeds with Calvin at this time is doubtful. Carried away by him, he sees a figure less reminiscent of the restrained author of the *Institutio christianae religionis* than of the writer of *Der Römerbrief* himself: 'Calvin is a cataract, a primeval forest, a demonic power, something directly drawn from Himalaya, absolutely Chinese, strange, mythological . . . . I could gladly and profitably set myself down and spend all the rest of my life just with Calvin' (p. 101). He had long admired Calvin as an expositor of the Scriptures; now he entered into the riches of the

Reformer's doctrine. The admiration was never a love, it was always tempered by a dislike of his personality. Nor did he ever become a devoted follower of Calvin's theology. In spite of an enviable acquaintance with his works and a profound understanding of his thought, he had no difficulty in standing on this side of idolatry.

At this stage his reading outside the Reformation was chiefly a preparation for understanding the Reformation. We hear talk of the later scholastics and of Bonaventure alone from the thirteenth century. Nothing from the early Church. Anselm does not now appear, but we note with interest that he has already helped in the revision of *The Epistle to the Romans*: 'I intend this very day [December 6, 1920] to look into the *Cur deus homo?* of Anselm' (p. 55). Cocceius and the federal theology of the seventeenth century enter at the end of 1922, when they pose the question as to who their modern descendants might be.

But what is Barth really doing in these two or three years? It is not simply a matter of a new professor feverishly compiling material for his lectures. The early years at Göttingen are decisive for the understanding of Barth's later course, and in particular of the *Church Dogmatics*. The complications are many. This enemy of the historical method is forced to learn history, and what is more, from the books of such exponents of that method as Harnack and Seeberg. He begins to take a modest pride in his craft as an historical theologian, a pride that makes him ashamed of his relative ignorance and wish that he knew more. 'I have to build my own scholarly structure, achieve a "thorough mastery" as they say, in *something*. How is one to do that? Will they ever be able to say that of me? Or shall I always be this wandering gypsy among all the honourable scholars by whom I am surrounded' (pp. 79-80). So he becomes an efficient professor. Yet he cannot forget the scorn with which Kierkegaard invested this word *professor*: 'The professor! This personage is not once mentioned in the New Testament — from which we can perceive first of all that Christianity came into the world without "professors". For the professor changes the whole point of view of Christianity' (*For Self-Examination*, p. 204). The problem was none the easier for being perceived in its true light. He had set himself against the general course of nineteenth century Protestantism. But the theological faculties were governed by the principles of this religion. But Barth had become a member of such a faculty. What, now, of all his talk of a great attack on the theologians, of his scepticism on Church history? What of Gogarten's renouncing the heritage of the nineteenth century? Where, now, is Overbeck? Where is Dostoevsky? Where is Blumhardt? Nay, which is more and most of all, where is Kierkegaard?

There were those who thought the whole Barthian movement was changing, or rather that its leaders were going over to the enemy. Hermann Kutter in Zürich, the venerable preacher of the social gospel, ever suspicious, wrote in sorrow to Thurneysen: 'The great task that we have in common, however weakly and falteringly we discharge it, of proclaiming God, is being made into a theology, a theological controversy — a ready meal for the theological eagles who are delighted that in disputing about the *concept* of God they may forget the striving after *God himself* (p. 210). Thurneysen replied gently, acknowledging that 'we have become ... theologians' (p. 213), but pleading that their whole intention is to build their theology on the Word of God. Barth is now too far on his road to be other than brusque: 'my answer would have proved somewhat uncivil' (p. 215).

To most eyes, however, Barth was still the author of *The Epistle to the Romans*. The revised edition was published within a month or two of his removal to Göttingen, became a best seller and was re-published at regular intervals until 1928. Nor did he write any other major work in this period which would divert attention from the commentary. *The Resurrection of the Dead*, an exposition of I Corinthians, appeared in 1924, but it is not equal to the Romans either in size or quality. We may suspect that it was based on work done on that epistle at Safenwil in 1919 (*Rev. Theol.* p. 48). Apart from this and the exposition of Philippians in 1927, lectures at Münster in 1926-27, nothing came from Barth's pen in these intermediate years but lectures and sermons.

A few of the lectures were transcripts of university lectures, like 'Schleiermacher's "Celebration of Christmas" ' and the more general 'Schleiermacher', but the most were delivered on lecture tours in Germany during these years. For Barth, the leader of the Dialectical Theology, was in great demand as a lecturer. Everybody wanted to see him, some wanted to hear him, not a few wanted to argue with him. So he went north, south, east and west, saw before him 'grave ministerial figures, excited young ones, blond-bearded liberals with glasses and those unfathomable German eyes behind them, indefinable, and, I must not forget, some enchanted ladies' (*Rev. Theol.* p. 107), made disciples to Barthianism, made enemies to Barthianism, showed some the way to read the Bible a bit differently, and was always 'the inveterate traveller with my little briefcase . . . back and forth from the express to the D-train, in waiting rooms and on station platforms with a pipe that rarely goes out' (p. 115). It is noteworthy how the substance of the lectures changes from the early prophesying in 1922 to historical lectures in 1923, 1924 and 1925. In 1922 occur some of the lectures that go to compose *The Word of God and the Word of Man*: 'The Need and Promise of Christian Preaching', 'The Problem of Ethics Today', and 'The Word of God and the Task of the Ministry'. In 1923, however, begins the series of substantial essays on the history of doctrine — 'Luther's Doctrine of the Eucharist', the two on Schleiermacher, 'Ludwig Feuerbach', 'The Word in Theology from Schleiermacher to Ritschl', 'The Principles of Dogmatics according to Wilhelm Herrmann'.

The lectures were not published as a collection until 1928, but they appeared individually in a periodical started and sponsored by Barth, Gogarten and Thurneysen and edited by Georg Merz, with the title taken from Gogarten's essay *Zwischen den Zeiten*. As we turn the pages of these old magazines we come upon the great names of the period who, to a greater or lesser degree, took the Barthian side. Rudolf Bultmann on eschatology in the Fourth Gospel, Hans Asmussen conducting a controversy with Werner Elert on Luther's theology and delivering the broadside: 'The basis of Elert's presentation is that of the theology of experience.' Barth's philosopher brother Heinrich and his Calvin-scholar brother Peter on their respective subjects.

Hermann Diem on Kierkegaard studies. Barth himself, Gogarten, Brunner, Thurneysen.

At the same time that Barth was learning theology, Barthianism was going from strength to strength, gathering adherents in Europe, Scandinavia, distant America. This was, however, small cause of self-congratulation to Barth. He looked with dismay at the popular movement that he had started, at the enthusiasm for negatives, the unthinking repetition of the catchwords — 'wholly Other', 'either-or', 'God is — God, and not man' and the rest. Nor were the theological relationships of the leaders of the movement running smoothly. Between Barth and Thurneysen the fellowship was sure. Brunner stood somewhat aside from them, and they permitted themselves to express doubts about him. Thurneysen, with keen eyes, notes that he says no important new thing, but that he is essentially right (*Rev. Theol.* p. 165). Within a year or two will appear the first of Brunner's majestic early volumes, *The Mediator*, and for a little while there will be no outward sign of division on this side. With Gogarten, however, things are different. Easy, of course, to be wise after the event, but how strange now seems Barth's belief that he and Gogarten were saying the same thing, even in the beginning, in the essay *Zwischen den Zeiten*. 'I am not at all of the opinion,' he wrote as late as 1923, 'that we are far distant from each other; on the contrary. From the lecture on the Apostles' Creed which I read beforehand, I am more than ever convinced that both of us are biting on the same bone' (pp. 121-2). And yet in the same letter he admits that he distrusts Gogarten. Earlier he had seen deeper into the trouble: 'The Christological problem is dealt with and solved by him with the help of a speculative I-Thou philosophy . . . . Heaven only knows where that will yet lead. Also in this respect I am really anxious about the future: Gogarten takes too *lofty* a position for me; when I listen to him I have always a desire to put myself on the side of the most uncomprehending historians' (p. 110). It may be that in this matter Barth was influenced against his better judgment by Thurneysen, who tried to interpret Gogarten to him as holding a position 'not so very different from ours' (p. 135). Certainly, he says, Gogarten's lack of a genuine eschatology leads to an apparent static quality in his statements. Certainly also, he stands at a dangerous point where he might all too easily lapse into mere Lutheranism. Nevertheless, his recent work is closer to the second edition of *The Epistle to the Romans*. Gogarten himself, however, also had his doubts, and in 1924 offered to drop off *Zwischen den Zeiten*. Barth would not permit this. They had got Gogarten and he was a useful ally against the "enemy". He would have done well to have agreed.

The Epistle to the Romans proved true to its name in another sense than the author had intended. There were not a few Roman Catholics who let it speak to them and who quickly perceived its significance. It must be remembered that the First Vatican Council of 1870 and the subsequent use made of its definition of Papal Supremacy had not only suppressed Liberal Catholicism but had also led to a firm closing of the Roman Catholic ranks against the other churches. So long as the leading representatives of Protestantism were liberals like Troeltsch, Harnack, and Wernle, there could be little interest in Protestantism for a Church which fundamentally held to belief in the continuing activity of the God who had revealed himself in his only-begotten Son. Protestantism had nothing to offer Rome; it provided no help in her inward questionings. But when *The Epistle to the Romans* appeared on the scene, the situation changed. It was from a Roman Catholic, Karl Adam, that the description came of this book as a bomb bursting in the playground of the theologians. And before long it was evident that Roman theologians, too, had been shaken by the blast. In 1924 Thurneysen reported the receipt of a 'remarkable article . . . by a Catholic writer . . . concerning our column, in which we are addressed as a partner in discussion to be taken seriously' (*Rev. Theol.* pp. 163f.). A few months later he is counselling a priest who contemplates leaving the Roman Church: 'For a start I have advised him to take his task and burden as a *Catholic* priest seriously and to remain in *his* church' (p. 205). Barth finds a Roman Catholic expounding Colossians and admitting his debt to him as one whom 'Catholic theology may not ignore without loss' (p. 180).

Barth has been taken by surprise at the reception. At first

he pretends it is all part of a devilish Roman plot that 'considers us ripe for capture' (p. 168); but in serious vein he wishes he could have a thorough talk with a well-instructed Jesuit. The Preface to the Fourth Edition of *The Epistle to the Romans* (1924) declares his appreciation of the Roman Catholic reviews, which 'have, for the most part, displayed a genuine understanding of the point at issue . . . . Now, what is the meaning of this fundamental, and to me quite unexpected, understanding? Erich Przywara, S. J., contrasts our "school"! with that of Otto and Heiler, judging it to be a "genuine rebirth of Protestantism". Joseph Engert, on the other hand, brings forward evidence to show that, apart from the doctrine of the Church elaborated in Chs. IX-XI, my commentary does not differ from the teaching of Thomas Aquinas, of the Council of Trent, and of the Roman Catechism . . . . The two reviewers are clearly not saying quite the same thing. Should they agree together as to what it is precisely they wish to say to us, we should be bound to answer them. Meanwhile, I cannot help saying that I regard it as a most hopeful sign for both sides that an opportunity should now be provided of entering into genuine theological, as opposed to merely historical, discussion with theologians of the Old Church' (*Romans*, p. 21).

It was characteristic of Barth that such a hope did not move him to accommodate his views towards the Roman position in the slightest. On the contrary, he both stated his own theology intransigently and pointed out bluntly what he considered the greater errors of Rome. In particular he accused her of holding a certain doctrine (*analogia entis*) in such a way as to admit a relationship of man with God apart from Jesus Christ. This doctrine, he said in the Foreword to *Church Dogmatics* I, 1, is 'the invention of Antichrist . . . because of it one cannot become Catholic' (p. X). Even these hard words were accepted in sorrow rather than anger, and learned essays were written to demonstrate that Barth had misunderstood the Roman doctrine, which was after all close to his own.

It would have seemed unbelievable in 1924 that within a generation loyal Roman Catholics, good theologians like Hans Urs von Balthasar, Henri Bouillard and Hans Küng would take the trouble to study and expound the work of this uncompromising Protestant. More, that they would compare his theology with that of their own Church and be ready to listen to him. For the first step on the path to reformation must be that a Church is willing to suspend its teaching for a time and instead just listen. Why has Rome listened to Barth? Not simply, as von Balthasar says, because he represents for the very first time in history genuine and pure Protestantism and because his theology is coextensive with Catholic theology. It is rather because the genuine and pure Protestantism that he represents is genuine and pure Catholicism. It was not that Protestants needed supplying with the Catholic element, or Catholics with the Protestant. No, both Catholics and Protestants needed to learn once again to become the Christian Church.

That so many Roman Catholics have listened to Barth is one of the miracles in the modern world. May it perhaps be that one of the reasons why the Second Vatican Council took place was that the ministers of Safenwil and Leutwil read their Bibles a little bit differently from the others?

All this, however, lay in the future, a consummation devoutly to be wished. For the present, Barth was struggling in his first academic post. By becoming a professor at Göttingen, Barth put himself into a difficult position in regard to his colleagues in the faculty. He was a Calvinist Daniel in a den of Lutheran lions. He came without academic experience; his chair was strictly speaking a minor one. But he was already well known, almost famous, throughout Europe. He was the centre of a great storm. He had written excessively severe things against historians and theologians. Small wonder that the other professors were suspicious. Small wonder, too, that they felt some jealousy when the students went to hear Professor Barth in greater numbers than to themselves, as Barth too gleefully reported to Thurneysen. Nor, unfortunately, was he at this time the man to smooth over such difficulties. Between Emmanuel Hirsch and himself there was in particular a mutual aversion. Hirsch also was new at Göttingen: but he had many years of teaching experience behind him. At first his assumption of superiority, of knowing what Barth had still to learn, was considerably irritating. After a little while, however, he was able to report to Thurneysen that 'relations with Hirsch are really good. Lively battles alternate with appointments for further meetings but the feeling remains intimate and stimulating. It is hard enough for me to swallow his eccentricities . . . but my varied ingredients are no less difficult to him . . . . If only some one of you could invite him to Switzerland for a couple of weeks in summer; he works himself into the ground so pitifully and he should really be preserved for the church for some years yet' (*Rev. Theol.* pp. 99-100). Can this be Barth? Can this be Hirsch? Alas! the sunshine did not last long, and a serio-comic theological thunderstorm in which Barth was rude to him, ended with Hirsch leaving the room 'with his dog following him most rapidly' (p. 142). Hirsch will reappear later in a more sinister light.

By 1924 Barth's relationship with the rest of the faculty 'is worse than ever', and he thinks 'it would be best if I could get away from this mousetrap' (p. 175). Where his path had led became clear as early as February 1924, when a storm blew up in the faculty over the title of his next course of lectures. He proposed: 'Prolegomena to Dogmatics', and after a fierce exchange issued the ultimatum that either it should be 'Instruction in the Christian Religion. Prolegomena' or he would appeal to the German Minister of Education. His appeal to the ministry, however, failed, and he was forced to accept the title 'Instruction in the Christian Religion'. But if he left Göttingen, where was he to go? Thurneysen suggested Kutter's church in Zürich. Barth thought he would be more fitted to the tiny village of Eriswil, a proposal that won only laughter in return. For some time there seemed a possibility that he might go to a chair in Bern, where his father had also been professor. In this uncertainty, Barth asked the university authorities what the Ministry of Education intended to do for him, and learned that he would probably shortly be invited to a chair at Münster-in-Westphalia. In July it was settled, and in October 1925 he moved into the new house in the street with the propitious name of Himmelreichsallee, "Kingdom of Heaven Avenue." But not before the students at Göttingen had shown their disagreement with the senior members and accorded him 'what usually happens only at the end of the second volume of the biography of great men, a full-scale *torchlight procession* of the whole theological student body' (*Rev. Theol.* p. 237).

The change of scene made little difference to Barth's inner theological development. Whether he was at Göttingen, Münster or Bonn, to which he removed in 1930, he pursued the same quest with essentially the same thread to guide him. The decisive change from Safenwil to Göttingen effected, we may pay less attention to the universities at which he held posts than to the broad fact that from 1921 to 1935 he was working in Germany and not in Switzerland, and also to the lines of study that he followed and the books that he read.

CHAPTER FOUR

A Fresh Beginning with Protestantism

AT GÖTTINGEN, CHIEFLY INSPIRED BY CALVIN, BARTH BECAME A systematic theologian. The immediate impetus was provided by the course of lectures on 'Prolegomena to Reformed Dogmatics' which he delivered early in 1924. He at once began to think and write of it as *Institutio*: 'I will interrupt for a while the profitable studies in which I have been engrossing myself in preparation for my Dogmatics, *alias Institutes of Christian Religion*' (*Rev. Theol.* p. 171). Calvin was at this time the model for his rethinking of dogmatic method. Not that he was making the *Institutio* the pattern for his own Dogmatics, but rather the model from which he would evolve a method. Now also he was working on Schleiermacher and particularly (in February 1924) *his* Dogmatics, *The Christian Faith*.

Three inter-connected problems intruded upon him. The first: What was the relation between the Reformation and Schleiermacher? How far and in what way was it responsible for the development that led to *The Christian Faith*? The second: Why did Schleiermacher and his theology exist at all? What was the purpose of God's providence in permitting this development to take place? And related to this, suppose that Schleiermacher's theology were taken completely out of the history of Protestantism, would there not be left a real gap, not just a barely noticeable crack in the wall? The third: If the first attempt, through its own fault, turned out badly, it follows that Protestantism now has the task 'to make a *fresh* beginning' (*Rev. Theol.* p. 175).

But at present he could not see the way to make a fresh beginning, although already he sensed that the secret lay within the doctrine of the Trinity. His immediate labour was to prepare for his lectures on dogmatics: 'All day long I am reading pell-mell hundreds and hundreds of pages: Heim, Thomas Aquinas, Fr. Strauss, Alex. Schweizer, Herrmann' (*Rev. Theol.* p. 176).

More important than this mélange, however, was his study in the early Church Fathers (the Apologists, Tertullian, Gregory of Nyssa, Athanasius — 'who must have been quite a man' — Augustine) and in the Calvinist and Lutheran schoolmen of the seventeenth and eighteenth centuries. He has left an account of how he first visited this last new world: 'I shall never forget the spring vacation of 1924. I sat in my study at Göttingen, faced with the task of giving lectures on dogmatics for the first time. No one can ever have been more plagued than I then was with the problem, Could I do it? And how? ... That Holy Scripture must be the controlling element in an evangelical dogmatics I also realised to the full. I was equally quite clear that the right thing was, in particular, to link up again with the Reformed .... But how to do it, without a guide? ... Then it was that, along with the parallel Lutheran work of H. Schmid, Heppe's [*Reformed Dogmatics*] just recently published fell into my hands; out of date, dusty, unattractive, almost like a table of logarithms, dreary to read, stiff and eccentric on almost every page I opened .... Well, I had the grace not to be slack. I read, I studied, I reflected' (*Heppe*, p. v). Here, he found to his surprise, was a more meaningful, a more reasonable, dogmatics than that provided by Schleiermacher or Ritschl, a dogmatics that was doctrinally turned towards the Scriptures and that continued the tradition of the early Church, the Middle Ages, the Reformation.

Moreover, Barth learned that theology could be, not merely exciting, but in its own right a beautiful science, a craft worth a man's labour. 'I had come to be amazed at the long, peaceful breathing, the sterling quality, the strict relevance, the superior style, the methods confident at least in themselves, with which this "orthodoxy" had wrought. I had cause for astonishment at its wealth of problems and the sheer beauty of its trains of thought .... In other words, I saw that Protestant dogmatics was once a careful, orderly business, and I conceived the hope that it might perhaps become so again' (*Heppe*, p. vi).

Many a wrong turning would still be taken, many a blind alley would force him to retrace his steps. It is one thing to wish to set Protestant theology on a fresh path and to hope for a renaissance of dogmatics. It is quite another to diagnose the precise weaknesses in Reformation theology that led to Schleiermacher and then to construct a theology that should not merely excise the faults but in its principles and methods and execution avoid both those faults and their opposites. Barth was not to find the way for another six or seven years. At the moment we see him endeavouring to discover it by wrestling with the doctrines themselves.

If *The Epistle to the Romans* was written with 'a joyful sense of discovery', no less joyfully now did he embrace the study of dogmatics. 'It pursues me even into my dreams' (*Rev. Theol.* p. 167). The letters are full of considerations of method, of the excitement of entering into new understandings of old doctrinal statements, of the joy of participating with the great doctors of the Church in their meditations. At first there is something of half-humorous reserve: 'I am just now in the midst of the mysteries of the Trinity. I had to think over it long and sadly, brooding ever and again over the runic characters which the ancients have left behind for us: *essentia, persona, notiones personales, opera ad intra — ad extra, perichoresis, "opera ad extra sunt indivisa"* (a thing perhaps to be considered, but all very complicated!) not to forget the *filioque* . . . . Don't think, however, that that is all old rubbish; all, all of it, seen in the light, seems to have its own good sense' (*Rev. Theol.* p. 185). Another year's study and reflection brings out the confession: 'I have finally to acknowledge that Orthodoxy is right on almost all points and to hear myself saying things in lectures which neither as a student nor as a Safenwil pastor would I ever have dreamed could really be so' (*Rev. Theol.* p. 221).

On the night of October 9, 1924, Karl Barth first thought of publishing his lectures on dogmatics as a book. At first, he hoped to bring out in 1925 the revision of a student's shorthand transcription of the lectures. Not all the transcription was made, however; nor was Barth in the end satisfied with the lectures. Publication was put off and put off for two years, until in 1927 appeared: *Christian Dogmatics in Outline*. Volume One: *The Doctrine of the Word of God. Prolegomena to Christian Dogmatics.*

There were to be two volumes. The first was a sizeable

book by usual standards, though but a pigmy in comparison with
what it was later to become. In the Foreword Barth reveals his
reasons for writing, and his purpose. There is also apparent
something of the uncertainty of this period of his life.

Many Dogmatics (he says) have been written in recent years
— by R. Seeberg, Lüdemann, Rade, Girgensohn, Wobbermin,
Stange, Herrmann, and Troeltsch. In at least one respect this
present Dogmatics differs from them all: it is not the fruit of a
life's work, but comes from the pen of a beginner. It is therefore
particularly open to correction. But I have undertaken it because
this seems the best way to carry on the discussions which have
arisen from earlier works by myself and my theological friends.
People have taken up our ideas and distorted them or treated
them one-sidedly. It will therefore be good if I discuss the whole
thing carefully and scientifically in the form of a Dogmatics.
Faced with the choice of writing in thirty years a respectable
and, it is to be hoped, learned and solid Dogmatics, or of doing
it now, in spite of manifold unpreparedness, yet as a younger
man to younger men and as questions and answers, I opt for
the second.

I feel self-conscious as a beginner in another sense too.
There is no place in modern Protestant dogmatics where I fit
in happily and honestly. Even the Dogmatics of my honoured
master, Wilhelm Herrmann, I can regard only as the final stage
of a development from which I must break away. It is true that
I am not cut off from all modern theology. I feel at home, for
varying reasons, in the company of the two Blumhardts, Dor-
ner, Kierkegaard, Kohlbrügge, Kutter, Müller, Overbeck, and
Vilmar, some of whom are almost, or quite, unknown today.
Apart from them, my teachers will be found only on the distant plains of history. So then, this *Dogmatics*, like *The Epistle
to the Romans* of eight years ago, treads a solitary path. I am
not proud of this fact, and those who think I am do little know
the problems it has caused me. For there is nothing in modern
dogmatics that I can use as a starting point. I myself have to begin everything from scratch. I know this is abnormal; but the
real cause for the abnormality lies in the false path that Prot-

estant dogmatics has been treading for at least two hundred years.

The whole of my *Dogmatics* I have called *Dogmatics in Outline*. A Dogmatics proper would be incomparably stricter, more methodical, complete and finished. This merely puts forward reflections and considerations in preparation for dogmatics. It is an attempt to catch sight once more of the problems of a genuine Dogmatics, without the intrusion of questions which have nothing to do with dogmatics.

Some of my friends are worried lest I should be turning into a dogmatician. Perhaps they will remind me of the beginning of my lecture on 'The Need and Promise of Christian Preaching' [*Word of God and Word of Man*, pp. 97ff.], and ask whether I am making a new theology out of the "marginal gloss" and the "corrective". Or it might be said that the threat of orthodoxy which many have seen hanging over me for a long time has now been realized. Perhaps they are lamenting that the spring-time of the "message of the Reformation" at which they thought they could rejoice in the 1922 *Epistle to the Romans* has been too quickly succeeded by a scholastic autumn. 'What reply shall I make? As I look back on my way, I see myself as a man feeling his way up the steps of a dark church tower. By mistake he lays hold of, not the hand-rail, but a rope, a bell-rope, and he has to listen, to his horror, to the great bell tolling above him for everyone to hear. He did not intend it. He has no wish to repeat it. In his confusion he will just go downstairs again as carefully as possible' (p. IX). It may be that my work has acted as a corrective, but that was not my intention. 'I was and I am a common or garden theologian' (p. IX). I feel no obligation or need to maintain the prophetic attitude in which some once saw me for a moment (and would like to go on seeing me all the time). I am not aware that I ever did anything but follow the pursuit of theology. For the future I have my path to tread on earth. And that means that I have to embark on my *Christian Dogmatics* without being able to ask what the outcome will be. Will the great bell ring again? What does that matter to me? My task, and my reader's, is to be occupied quite unassumingly with the material of dogmatics.

This first attempt at a Dogmatics is marked by a combination of power and uncertainty. It would have been impossible for Barth to write in anything but a firm and urgent manner, drawing into the light the main points in every topic, showing the way which the arguments should take, making the reader a participant in the drama of faith or of understanding. So much we expect from Barth, and rarely are we disappointed. But in *Christian Dogmatics* there is also an undertone of uncertainty quite foreign to him, far removed from the atmosphere of either of the commentaries on Romans or of the later *Church Dogmatics*. It betrays itself sometimes in the language. Take this revealing word with which he begins the book: *Bemühung*. *Bemühung* comes from a noun which means "trouble", "labour", "toil", "effort". It is related to the adjective *müde*, "weary", "fatigued". And *Bemühung* itself signifies "exertion" or "endeavour". Yet this inauspicious word is applied to dogmatics as its task: 'We call dogmatics the *Bemühung* to reach the knowledge of the legitimate content of Christian speech about God and man.' And all through this first section *Bemühung* is drummed in as the work of dogmatics. We might be forgiven for thinking that it sounds as if Barth has had such a hard grind over the last five years learning dogmatics that the iron has eaten into his soul. And yet how happily he will write, even in the midst of stressing *Bemühung*: 'What we today call dogmatics was for a Thomas or a Bonaventure quite seriously also a beautiful and joyful work of art. Thomas could envisage the genuine doctors of the Church wearing heavenly crowns along with the martyrs and virgins' (p. 6).

But it is the substance of the book that will present the surprises. A section on "The Word of God as Revelation" will not mention Jesus Christ once, but will get itself entangled in a generalizing and therefore not wholly accurate study of the sixteenth century Reformed view of the relationship between revelation and the words of Scripture. Or what are we to make of such a title as 'God in the Sermon' (§23, p. 411), followed by the stark assertion, 'God's Word is God in the Church's proclamation' (p. 411)? Or take the titles of the first two parts of §7: '1. Faith or God's Word? 2. God's Word and faith.' This represents the sort of ideas that, if he had found them in another theologian, he might well have quoted with relish and several exclamation marks in a letter to Thurneysen. Indeed, in *Christian Dogmatics* he wrote some things that later surprised even himself, so that we find him referring in *Church Dogmatics* I,1 to an "astonishing" statement he had perpetrated on p. 111.

In particular there were three whole sections (§§ 5-7) that offended. When we set them in the context of Barth's whole argument, their fault stands out starkly. Chapter I is intended to lay the foundations of the book, and it has therefore a special importance. Dogmatics is the task of understanding and correcting the Church's preaching about God. Dogmatics is based on the Word of God, its source and its norm. Chapter I, then, entitled 'The Reality of the Word of God', lays this foundation by describing the nature of the Word of God on which the rest of the book depends. The first two sections (§§ 3-4) are not substantially very different from §§ 3-4 of *Church Dogmatics* I, 1. The complex of Church proclamation, language about God, the Word of God, and their relation to dogmatics are explored in § 3; while in § 4 the three-fold form of the Word of God as proclamation, canon, and revelation is laid down. All this, be it noted, deals with what is objective — preaching, Bible, revelation in events. But § 5, 'The Word of God and man as preacher', opens ominously with a subsection called 'An Alteration in the Mode of Consideration'. Hitherto, says Barth, we have been treating everything phenomenologically — that is, by way of looking at objects outside ourselves. Revelation, however, means not only that God reveals himself, but that he reveals himself by certain means and to men. Revelation does not occur in a vacuum but in concrete situations. It is to be understood existentially: men preach, men listen, men believe. The preaching, listening and believing are important parts of revelation and therefore the Word of God upon which dogmatics is based. Hence a part of the foundation of dogmatics consists in examining and explaining man's experience of the Word of God.

Extraordinary! We are back almost with Schleiermacher, whom we thought we had bidden goodnight. What has happened? Has Barth on reflection decided that, in regard to the objectivity of revelation, he has been wrong, and that a place must be given in the foundation of theology to man's religious experience? Or is this an element which he had not yet eliminated from his thinking? It is not so simple a matter as that, for Barth is here giving expression to views which he had ceased to hold long since and which he had rejected in earlier writings. What is the 1922 *Epistle to the Romans* but a concentrated attack on the religion of experience? If he had not set himself to think through and systematize what he already held, he would not have found himself at these surprising conclusions. We are closer to the truth if we say that he was led astray by a faulty method. Yet even this is not quite accurate. It was not that his method was basically faulty in itself, but that he had not made it consistent with itself, and he did not see how to adapt it and apply it to the various topics. Above all, at this point he allowed another method, a philosophical method, to take control.

What was needed, as he soon came to see when criticism after criticism was levelled against these sections, was a thorough reconsideration of his dogmatic method.

CHAPTER FIVE

The Quest for Understanding

BARTH HAD PUBLISHED THE FIRST VOLUME OF HIS *Christian Dogmatics*. He could not deny that he was to blame when it was misinterpreted. Some seven years earlier he had been inwardly compelled to rewrite *The Epistle to the Romans*; now it became clear to him that he must make a fresh start with the Dogmatics when the first edition was sold out. It was not that he wished to correct the substance but that he knew that he had pursued a wrong course in his method: 'I could and I wanted to say the same thing as before; but now I could no longer say it in the way in which I had said it before.' His problem was how to base theology on God's self-revelation alone and preserve the character of revelation as genuinely historical event, how to write about faith, experience, belief, the knowledge of God, without making them an independent basis for theological thinking. Just as faith depends entirely on its object, so the knowledge which is inherent in faith and towards which faith moves must depend entirely upon its object, not upon itself or upon the faith with which it is related. He knew, and he had known for years, that this must be so. But how it could be so without the knowledge ceasing to be genuine human knowledge, he did not yet know.

The key for which he had been seeking was discovered as he prepared for a seminar at Bonn in the summer of 1930. The subject of the seminar was the book by the eleventh century Archbishop of Canterbury, Anselm: *Cur deus homo — Why the God-man* or *Why God became man*. Anselm had long been a favourite with Barth — we see him having recourse to the *Cur deus homo* at Safenwil. For his seminar Barth prepared by an extensive course of reading of Anselm, *Cur deus homo, Monologion, Proslogion*, the prayers, the meditations, the letters, the theological treatises. As he read, Anselm's method became clear

69

to him as a method that based theological thinking only upon its object and yet preserved its rationality.

He at once wrote a book on Anselm's method, which was published in 1931 as *Anselm: Fides Quaerens Intellectum. Anselm's Proof of the Existence of God in the Context of his Theological Scheme*. This is perhaps Barth's greatest work, his most important contribution to theological literature. It need not surprise us that it is also the least read of his major books and was not even reprinted until 1958, for this is also the hardest of all Barth's works to understand, whether in German or in the English translation. Indeed, to use mountaineering language, if the climb is very difficult in German, in English it is severe. We would therefore recommend to any reader who knows also some German to have constant recourse to the original. He will find it easier than trying to understand the English on its own. But if Barth's theology is really to be comprehended, *Fides Quaerens Intellectum* must first be mastered; and if now we are to plot Barth's theological course aright, we cannot omit a description of the book, leaving a patch of white *terra incognita* behind us on the map. 'In this book on Anselm I am working with a vital key, if not the key, to an understanding of that whole process of thought that has impressed me more and more in my *Church Dogmatics* as the only one proper to theology' (*Fid. Quaer. Int.* E.T. p. 11).

One more preliminary word. In what follows it is completely irrelevant for our purpose whether Barth is interpreting Anselm aright or no. Our sole interest is in what he understood Anselm to be saying, and thus in his discovery of a method for his own work.

'Faith's search for understanding': that was Anselm's concept of theology. It was a concept that summed up the New Testament teaching on faith, knowledge and love, the strivings of the early Church Fathers to relate trust and assent to cognition. Faith has embarked on the quest for understanding. But why? What force drives faith out and on? It is true that there is really quite a simple and even banal reason. On the one hand, unbelievers and heretics have to be silenced with good, strong arguments. On the other, the waverers and the fearful in mind have to be convinced of the truth; and this, too, needs good, strong arguments. But such theological warfare and first aid work is only incidental. Anselm sees another aim in the quest of faith, and that is that the believer may have joy in understanding. The quest is therefore not only utilitarian, but also takes place in the realm of beauty and delight.

Not that the question has now been answered. Faith does not seek for joy or for the delight of beauty. This would be a perverted knowledge for the sake of knowledge rather than for the sake of the object. Yet the clue has been given. Why is faith impelled to seek understanding? Not simply for its usefulness in polemics or apologetics. Joy, beauty, delight — all this means freedom and spontaneity, in fact, desire. There is 'a spontaneous desire of faith' (p. 16) to seek understanding, a compulsion that is not imposed from without but is immanent in faith. Why must faith seek understanding? Just because it is faith.

From this follows something of crucial importance in the relationship of faith and understanding. Theology, the quest for understanding, is not intended to create faith, confirm faith, or overcome doubt, whether for the theologian himself or for others. The existence of faith remains unaffected by the success or failure of theological investigation. It is faith seeking understanding, not understanding seeking faith. If faith gains its desire for understanding, it is crowned with joy; if it fails to attain understanding of the Truth, then it remains faith and bows in reverence before the Truth which it believes but does not understand. 'Therefore, just because we possess the certainty of faith, we must hunger after faith's reason' (p. 21).

Yet not all human desires are capable of attainment. Faith may wish for understanding; but is understanding possible for faith? If faith itself were an irrational urge towards God, the swing of the compass to the north, the migration of birds to warmer lands, then the desire for understanding would be neither possible nor necessary. But faith is not irrational; it comes from hearing human words which represent the Word of Christ; it is conceived by the Word of Christ; it corresponds to the Word of Christ. Therefore, as the Word of Christ is truly and genuinely rational, so that which is conceived by it and corresponds to it cannot be irrational. If, however, faith is not 'illogical, irrational, and wholly deficient in knowledge' (p. 22), it follows that faith itself has from the outset a certain understanding. We may go further and say that faith is never without knowledge.

The direct object of faith is what Anselm calls 'the Word of Christ', and which he glosses as 'the words of those who preach Christ' (p. 22, n. 3). But "preach" must not mislead us into thinking of wandering medieval friars or the Sunday pulpit diet of today. It refers to the Bible taken together with the Creeds, the Fathers (especially Augustine) and the decision of the Pope; that is, the Bible and the confession of the Church. At this point Barth dissociates himself from Anselm, for whom, four and a half centuries before the Reformation, the relationship of Bible and tradition was no problem. Nevertheless, the point at issue does not concern the scope of "the Word of Christ" but "the Word of Christ" itself. Faith has as its direct object "the Word of Christ" in the confession of the Church. Its object is the concrete message of the Church, bearing witness to the Truth. Therefore faith is also an assent to the message, an acknowledgment of its truth. And when we say that, we are again saying that faith has at the outset a certain understanding.

What is this initial understanding? In the first place, quite simply, it is the understanding of the message as a piece of human speech. It is a linguistic and grammatical understanding. Such a comprehension is not peculiar to faith. The unbeliever can attain it as easily as the believer. The understanding of faith is more than this, for it is assent to the truth of the message. But now, the Truth is the goal of faith's quest. Therefore, ultimate knowledge is anticipated at the very start of faith. The end is contained in the beginning. Certainly, there is a difference between assent and the fruition of understanding. But it is one of degree only. Faith is a primitive understanding. And so faith's search for understanding does not involve it in a long journey, a search far and wide for the Holy Grail of knowledge, but only in exploring a certain tract of country which it already inhabits. This tract of country lies between two events which have occurred — the grammatical comprehension of the message and the grasp and affirmation of its truth. This tract of country is the realm of theology, of faith seeking understanding. And because faith itself also has the character of knowledge and its object is the true Word of Christ in the proclamation of the Church, the search is a practicable proposition, theology is possible.

From here we have to go on to the terms of theology. A man, before he takes up a job, will settle the terms of his employment with his employer. Usually he will not be free to do just what he likes, but will have certain duties assigned to him. Theology, too, has its terms of employment.

(1) The task of understanding is bound to the Church's confession of faith. If faith is assent to this confession or *Credo*, how could its search be conducted apart from or in opposition to that confession? So theology does not question the truth of the confession, but after-thinks it. (I trust the reader will not be too harsh on this weird verb "after-thinks", more befitting the pages of Thomas Carlyle than, I hope, these. The usual English translations for this word, e.g. "meditate", "contemplate", "ruminate", do not bring out what I think Barth means). Faith assents to the truth of the confession; it seeks to understand this truth by thinking again the thoughts of the confession. It does not indulge in "free-thinking", but is bound to the confession; it thinks *after* the confession, just as the disciple follows *after* his master. On the other hand, it does not simply repeat the thoughts of the confession, but re-thinks them — yet the re-thinking does not contradict the truth of the confession. It starts from, is accompanied by, and moves towards that truth.

(2) The task of theology is to ask about the nature of the truth believed. From the confession faith conceives the truth. To what extent does this conception correspond to the truth of the confession? But at once a danger becomes apparent. If we are not careful, we shall soon be asking whether it corresponds at all, and that means substituting doubt for faith, something that is already ruled out. Theology therefore has a limit set to its operation, beyond which it may not pass, and indeed will not pass if it is *faith* seeking understanding. The limit is marked out by the twin questions: Is the truth in the confession really the Truth? Is faith really more than an opinion, really the certainty corresponding to the divine Truth? When it comes up against

the limit set by these questions, all theology can do is to grasp and express in a rational manner the incomprehensibility of God's revelation and the miracle of faith.

(3) There is no perfection or finality about theological statements. They are all inadequate to express the truth about God. For the only one who can have conceptions of God is God himself. All we can conceive are objects which are not God and which are not equivalent to God. The ways in which we try to understand God are not the way in which he knows himself. How, then, can it be said that it is possible to attain to understanding at all? Because there are objects which, although they are not identical with God, serve as genuine similitudes or images. They are like mirrors. We look at a mirror and see someone's face. The mirror is certainly not their face. We are not looking at their face but at the mirror. And yet we see their face and can make a statement about it which can more or less correspond to the truth. Nevertheless, such a statement will still be inadequate when it is a question of God and the things which are not God by which he reveals himself.

(4) There follows from this the degree of certainty that belongs to theological statements. They do not have the absolute assurance of faith, but only the relative certainty which all scientific results possess. The theologian cannot speak as if his understanding were itself the truth or had the authority of its object. On the contrary, the uniqueness and sovereignty of that object will only serve to highlight the relativity of even his sublimest concepts, his profoundest insights. A great deal of his work will therefore be experimental and provisional, not merely accepting, but inviting, criticism. He will not assume that he is right, but will be only too keenly aware of the feeblemindedness of his efforts. But what about when he quotes Scripture or says in his own words precisely the same thing as Scripture? The Church's confession certainly stands above this relative certainty. But quoting or repeating Scripture is not the exercise of understanding; theology begins where this ends.

(5) In this world theology is never a perfect and so a completed achievement. The greatest theologies — Athanasius, Augustine, Anselm, Aquinas, Luther, Calvin — are capable of im-

provement and advance. It is not simply a case of some truths being hidden on earth and revealed only in heaven. There are some truths and methods which have been and are still hidden, but which are capable of being understood on earth, and which in the wisdom of God will be grasped in his own good time. We are here dealing with the progress of theology.

(6) By what criterion, however, are we to judge whether the "new" theologies really represent a progress of theology or an aberration? Ultimately only God knows this, for only God knows God. And since God cannot be appealed to for his verdict, theology is a very vulnerable science. Earlier, however, we learned that Scripture is the source of faith's understanding. Therefore it is also the criterion by which new departures are to be judged. So long as they do not contradict the teaching of Scripture, they must be admitted as valid.

(7) Theology is not a purely intellectual exercise. It springs from faith, it is moved throughout by faith. Theology is *faith* seeking to understand. Therefore there can be no correct knowledge when faith is lacking. A false faith or no faith at all impairs the scientific nature of theology just as surely as does a faulty method or wrong conclusions. The theologian must therefore have a genuine faith which is directed towards its unique object. 'What is required is a pure heart, eyes that have been opened, child-like obedience, a life in the Spirit, rich nourishment from Holy Scripture to make him capable of finding these answers' (p. 34).

(8) Again, if theology is faith seeking to understand, it means that the understanding comes in answer to prayer, for prayer is the exercise, the practice, of faith. But if in answer to prayer, then it is a gift of God. There are two senses in which this is true. The first, quite straightforwardly, is that the understanding of the truth is not the achievement of the unaided human reason, but is given by God. It is a gift of grace that a man shall follow the correct theological reasoning through to its conclusion. This grace the theologian must seek by prayer. In the second sense, we are taken to the very gates of the sanctuary. What is it that God gives? Not only this or that gift which he knows to be necessary for a man, but comprehensively himself.

The understanding that faith seeks is the knowledge of God, not simply knowledge about God. 'It is not just a question here of the right way to seek God, but also, along with this, of God's presence, which is basically the whole grace of Christian knowledge, and of the encounter with him which cannot be achieved by our seeking of God, however pure it might be — although it only happens to him who seeks God with a pure heart' (p. 38). That God will make himself the object of his thinking and thus will make the thinking a genuine understanding of the Truth, must be the prayer of the theologian. Faith prays for understanding, and seeks for understanding, and prays that its search for understanding may be crowned by the knowledge of God.

These are the terms under which theology works.

The Latin word that Anselm used for "understand" is *intelligere*. This comes from two words, *intus legere*, which mean literally "to read within". It is this idea which forms the starting point for the next section on the path that theology treads.

We have already heard about the reading part of the *intus legere* — that is, Holy Scripture, to which faith and understanding are committed. Indeed, the process of understanding consists in "thinking after" the Scripture, which is the centre of the Church's confession or *Credo*. Another way of expressing "thinking-after" is "reading within". There is nothing superficial about the understanding which faith seeks. It does not merely consist in reading the Bible and understanding the words, sentences, paragraphs, histories, and concepts. By grace, in faith, it penetrates within to the meaning of the Bible and thinks about that meaning. For there are two depths to be read in the Bible, just as there are two depths of reading. There is the level of the words and the histories and the concepts. But there is also the level of the truth of the Bible. And this level demands the "reading-within", the *intelligere*, the understanding. The spatial metaphors are misleading, for the deeper level, or inward meaning, exists only in the outward text. Nor does the inward meaning say anything different from, or, indeed, anything more profound than the outward text. It exists in the outward text, but it is not read when that is read; it has to be sought deliberately, and it can only be found as God gives it to be found.

This means that the method of using passages of Scripture as authoritative proof-texts is inadmissible. For these same passages are, of course, the outward text which has to be understood; and if it has to be understood, how can it support as proof the result of understanding? Theology begins where Scripture ends; it is "after-thinking". To quote proof-texts is not therefore to clinch the argument finally, but only to state the initial problem again. Anselm himself is remarkably sparing of quotations from the authorities — Bible, Creeds, Fathers. He does not substitute "It is written" for scientific enquiry. Understanding is given by God as a man meditates upon this or that part of the Church's confession, examining its meaning in isolation and also in relation to other articles, comparing them, connecting them, and so allowing them to shed light upon one another.

What has Barth achieved in his investigation, whether it is a faithful representation of Anselm or not? He has established a method in theology that does justice to its subject, as any method must if it is to be both workable and fruitful. It preserves the incomprehensibility of God's self-revelation while insisting that it is genuine unveiling; it makes faith a genuine human experience, knowledge of God a genuinely rational exercise, while insisting that they are the gift of God. We should be careful how we think of a theological method, however. Barth has not established a central principle from which he can work out all his doctrines, nor cut a key which will open all the doctrinal doors. It is not even a matter of a vantage point from which the theological landscape may be viewed. It is rather a way of examining and understanding doctrines and concepts.

The heart of the method which he has evolved lies in the relationship between faith and its object (and what is true of faith is true also of understanding and knowledge). The object of faith is not made true by the genuineness or sincerity of that faith. We may put a whole-hearted trust in a man's promise; but this will not make his promise sincere. On the opposite hand, faith is made true by the truth of its object. The least and most timorous bit of trust in someone's promise is abundantly justified if the promise is honoured. We may go further and say that faith (whether belief or trust) is created by its object. Faith and understanding really are human activities, and yet they derive from their objects — that God is our Saviour in Jesus Christ and that he gives himself to be known. To put it comprehensively, faith and understanding correspond to their object.

Now, if this is so, it follows that we may not base a theology on the sincerity, or depth, or correctness of faith in itself. For this will, by itself, tell us nothing about its object, but only about itself. The basis for theology must be the object itself.

Theology is therefore differentiated from philosophy, which obeys other laws and which demands a free thinking. Therefore, if the theologian introduces philosophy in his attempt to understand, he steps right aside from his theological pursuit. This was Barth's error in the *Christian Dogmatics*, when he attempted to understand faith by means of an existentialist philosophy. When the theologian makes use of philosophical language or concepts he must be careful that they do not take control and determine the nature either of the understanding or its object.

The starting point and guiding line and goal of theology must be the object which faith seeks to understand. And that is? The object of faith is God himself. The first facet of the method of theology is that it is turned towards God. This orientation does not exclude consideration of other entities than God; but it does exclude a turning away from God in order to consider them.

God, however, "dwells in light inaccessible", he is known only to himself. Yet in his great mercy he makes it possible for man to know him by means of that which *can* be the object of man's cognition. God reveals himself in the life, death and resurrection of the man Jesus. Apart from him he is completely unknown and unknowable. In him, he makes himself into the object of man's faith and understanding. The second facet of the method of theology is that it is turned towards Jesus Christ. And here we stand at the heart of the matter. Jesus Christ, the God-man, is the object of faith and the object of faith's understanding. This orientation also does not exclude consideration of other entities besides Jesus Christ; but it does exclude a turning away from him in order to consider them. Hence, theology will be always an attempt to understand in the light of Jesus Christ.

Jesus Christ, however, is not just a concept or a principle. He is the one whose history is narrated and interpreted in certain documents — that is, the Bible. This is who Jesus Christ is. Therefore, when we say that Jesus Christ is the object of faith and the object of understanding, we mean that the object of faith and understanding is the one whose history is narrated and interpreted in the Bible. It follows that the Bible becomes the object (in a somewhat different sense) of faith and understanding — that is, that it is trusted as the reliable narrator and interpreter of Jesus Christ and studied in the attempt to arrive at an understanding of Jesus Christ.

The history of Jesus Christ is not simply the history of a man. The Jesus Christ of the Bible is the God-man, and his history is the self-revelation of the incomprehensible God. The witness of the Bible to him is not simply a biography but a confession of faith in him. The Biblical writers believed in him and knew him by the illumination of the Holy Spirit and not by their own perception. Hence, the Bible is seen in two lights as the object of faith and understanding. As an historical document it is the object of credence and investigation like any other document. But as the believing witness to God's self-revelation in Jesus Christ, it is the object of faith in Jesus Christ as God's self-revelation. The third facet of the method of theology is therefore that theology is turned towards the believing witness of the Bible. This orientation also does not exclude the consideration of other entities than this witness; but it does exclude a turning away from it in order to consider them.

We come to the faith that seeks to understand. It is faith in the incomprehensible God in his self-revelation in Jesus Christ in the believing witness of the Scriptures. Faith, however, is determined by its object and corresponds to it. Faith therefore has a correspondence (not an identity) with the incomprehensible God in his self-revelation in Jesus Christ in the believing witness of the Scriptures. It therefore partakes of the truth and the certainty of its object. The fourth facet of the method of theology is that the faith from which it starts and by which it is all the time motivated is determined by and corresponds to its object.

In *Fides Quaerens Intellectum* Barth has halted the course of Protestant theology and changed its direction. His own course since about 1916 has not been changed by *Fides Quaerens Intellectum*, however. His mind has been clarified, his thinking has been ordered; but the problems which he has now settled are basically the same problems that have exercised him all along, and the solution to the problems is but the extension and clarification of the solution he had reached before *The Epistle to the Romans*. After the last war it was said that Barth had changed. He himself, in his humorous way, insisted that he was "still the same old Barth". And he was right, not only in regard to the later situation, but fundamentally also to his whole working life, which was a paradox of movement and fixity. Critics were forever complaining that, like Browning's Waring, "he gave us all the slip". A position he held or a piece of terminology he had used would be attacked; but it was too late; he had already struck camp and moved from that position, abandoned that terminology. And yet at the same time he held from first to last the one central position from which he never shifted.

So it is here. Let us cast our minds back to Chapter I and the theologians to whom the young Barth was heir. Schleiermacher with his view of theology as faith, Christian experience, seeking to understand itself. Ritschl and the historical method of Bible study. Herrmann's lectures on dogmatics: God is incomprehensible, he is hidden even in his revelation. Against Schleiermacher Barth had insisted that the object of faith was of primary importance, the subjective experience of faith secondary. Now in 1931 it is still a question of faith seeking understanding. To that extent Barth is a fellow-worker with Schleiermacher, who had quoted on the title page of his *Christian Doctrine* the similar saying from Anselm: "I believe in order that I may understand". But faith is not searching for its own nature, theology is not faith looking at itself in a mirror. What faith seeks to understand is its object, God in Jesus Christ witnessed to by the Scriptures. Against the Ritschlian school Barth had insisted that the historical method is only the first step in the understanding of the Bible, and that the proper understanding of the Bible is spiritual — and had been called a spiritualizing enthusiast for his pains, a Marcion, a Thomas Münzer. Now in 1931 it is still a question of the two levels of Scripture, of the inner text within the outer, of the linguistic and grammatical understanding and the understanding which is assent to its truth. And Herrmann? 'I let Herrmann say to me one essential truth': 'The Christian's religious knowledge begins with the group of obvious facts . . . but it ends with the confession that the God whose innermost nature has become revealed to us as love, still remains for us a God enthroned in unapproachable light'. The first part of *Anselm: Fides Quaerens Intellectum* is an island where we are never out of hearing of the waves of Wilhelm Herrmann beating on the shore.

Fides Quaerens Intellectum was not a turning point in Barth's theological career; rather it represented a crystallization of his thinking which made possible his later work. From this severely academic book sprang not only the *Church Dogmatics* but also his gift to the German Confessing Church of its theological foundation; from it sprang, too, the controversy with Brunner, as well as Barth's books on the Creeds and the Confessions of Faith. From it came, if I am not mistaken, Barth's understanding of the music of Mozart.

In the history of theology, the achievement of *Fides Quaerens Intellectum* cannot be over-rated. 'What a task then it is to make a *fresh* beginning once more with Protestantism' (*Rev. Theol.* p. 175). The "method" set out in this book in no way contradicts the particular insights of the Reformation but insists on them more rigorously and consistently than the Reformers themselves had done. Every one of the "facets" of theological method were commonplaces to the Reformers, and, indeed, controlled their theology in general. But they did not think them through consistently. The result was that even Calvin, the greatest systematic theologian of the century, could commit in the *Institutio christianae religionis* similar faults to those found in the *Christian Dogmatics* — and, unfortunately, not correct them five years later. Luther had re-discovered the Augustinian understanding of faith as the gift of God corresponding to the grace of God in Jesus Christ justifying a man and issuing in love. Luther taught the Church the meaning, so to say, of *fides quaerens caritatem*, faith seeking love. Neither he nor Calvin, nor any other of the Reformers, however, applied the same principle to doctrine. The greatness of Barth's achievement is that what Luther did in the moral sphere, he accomplished in the intellectual. The Roman Catholics are right when they say that in Barth the principles of the Reformation are fully realized for the first time.

CHAPTER SIX

The One Word of God

THE FIRST FRUIT OF BARTH'S NEW UNDERSTANDING OF THEOLOGICAL method was the revision of his *Dogmatics*, on which he entered at once, and the first volume of which he published in 1932. But the forward course of the work was halted by political events. He was working in Germany, in the Germany which, within a year, was to become the Third Reich governed by Adolf Hitler. Barth had known the old Germany before the Great War; he had lived through the post-war years of economic depression and political unrest; now he was to suffer the Germany of National-Socialism.

When he moved to Göttingen in 1921 he was caught into the depression. 'The constantly deteriorating condition of the economy' (*Rev. Theol.* p. 118) not only depressed but personally affected him. It was a sign of the times that the third edition of *The Epistle to the Romans* (1922) brought him in half a million marks, enough, he wrote wistfully to Thurneysen, to have set him up with a house and car in the old days. Six months later he is a millionaire, with an annual stipend of six million marks. But as by September 1923 a cup of coffee costs four million marks, he can hardly be placed in the higher income bracket. His post was not a full professorship, and commanded a correspondingly lower stipend. There seems, indeed, to have been a time two years later when he was in financial difficulties. Certainly the congregation of a Reformed church in northeast Germany sent him a gift of eight hundred marks on hearing such a rumour in 1925 (the monetary system had by now steadied, and the sum was quite a respectable one). Whether there was a basis for the rumour, I do not know; one would have thought that the books, and in particular *The Epistle to the Romans*, would be bringing in a steady income.

In the letters of this time there may be heard too, some

83

mutterings of the nationalist storm. The dedication of the Göttingen war-memorial in 1924 was an early warning which Barth
noted in a letter: 'It was quite worthwhile for me to see the
Wilhelmian Germany, i.e., the German-national-racial Germany,
gathered for once in one place . . . all of them gave their speeches:
"Young heroes — August, 1914 — Germany in the heart and on
the lips — the individual must die that the state may live — they
have entered Valhalla — they live eternally in our hearts — shame-
ful peace of Versailles — November men of 1918 — true to the
death — better times — when the next war comes — property
and life — what young German heart would not — German oak
woods — victor in a thousand battles — fallen heroes — you too
will" . . . in general I cannot deny that the whole phenomenon
and the possibility which it evidently embodies has made an impression upon me, so that when it is all over I am glad I did not
play truant from the whole hullaballoo, bad as it all was' (*Rev.
Theol.* p. 194). Before eight years were fulfilled, this nationalism
had advanced from the yearly Armistice service speech and inward aspirations to bearing sovereign rule in the daily life of
Germany.

The ideas and aims of National-Socialism, patriotic, clear-
cut, practical, were a word of salvation to a Germany defeated
in war, humiliated in peace, and broken in her economy. A
church is a part of the society within which it exists, is affected
by its troubles and by its recoveries. When that church is the
church of Martin Luther, the great German, and has a long history
of the closest association with the state, then it will be touched
very near by every vicissitude of the nation. Nationalism was now
intensified by the National-Socialist doctrine of purity of race,
proclaimed with emotional fervour but little scientific accuracy.
They were true Germans in whose veins flowed "Aryan" blood.
The others, even those who could not boast four pure-blooded
non-Aryans as grandparents, were at best second-class citizens.
The old German legends, the old German heroes, the old German songs and customs, were pressed into service. How could the
German Church fail to be touched by such a movement? 'Be
pious; be German; and the living God will give you your daily

bread' (Bishop Hossenfelder, quoted in A. Keller: *Religion and the European Mind*, p. 114).

But it is of the highest importance to note that the religious doctrines in National-Socialism were not derived from the Lutheran Church, but were considerably older than Christianity itself. The very term "Aryan" betrays everything. We are transported back into an Eastern thought-world of pantheism, of natural religion, of man's self-redemption from darkness and nothingness, of man's identity with God. To all this was joined the religion of the old Northern sagas, and the result was grafted into Christianity by such writers as Rosenberg, with his *Myth of the Twentieth Century*. But it could only be grafted in if parts of Christianity were taken out, and essential parts at that. Jesus Christ ceases to be the suffering Lamb of God, despised and rejected, and becomes the Hero, the Leader, the Light-bringer. The Old Testament, the book of the non-Aryan Jews, must be dropped from the sacred literature of Christians to make way for the sacred Aryan ideas.

Looking back over the years, knowing what these ideas led to, remembering the heroic resistance of a Niemöller, a Schneider, or a Bonhoeffer, we are shocked to the core that any educated Christian should lend an ear to such unchristian nonsense. We forget that there were many, in Britain and America as well as in Germany, who saw good in what was happening, who could agree with W. M. Horton of Oberlin College when he wrote: 'Those who are unreservedly opposed to [Barth's] theology will have to make an attempt to appreciate the truth in the German Christian Movement. Personally, I believe there *is* truth in it' (*Contemporary Continental Theology*, p. 107).

The German Christian Movement was already in existence when Adolf Hitler and the Nazi movement came to power in January 1933. It had existed since 1930 as the Christian German Movement, having among its leaders Emmanuel Hirsch of Göttingen. The programme of the movement had been — and continued to be — that National-Socialism was the summons of God to the German people to renew their faith. In keeping with the anti-Communist character of Nazism there was envisaged a mighty conflict between the forces of atheistic Marxism and National-

Socialism in which was subsumed the Christianity of the German Church. It is said to have been Hitler himself who gave the movement its new name of German Christian. Their leader, Hossenfelder, was made adviser for church affairs in the Ministry of Education in January 1933, but his dominant position was very soon transferred to the Army chaplain, Ludwig Müller, who enjoyed, moreover, access to the Führer.

In May there was constituted a committee to reorganize and unify the German Churches (that is, broadly speaking, the Lutheran and Reformed Churches). The committee consisted of a Lutheran, a Reformed, and the President of the Church Federation. When Müller was added to their number as a sort of adviser and observer, he was welcomed and treated as a full member. The reorganisation of the unified Church took the form of government by a national bishop (*Reichsbischof*), local bishops in the regional churches, and a National Synod. Müller claimed the post of *Reichsbischof* for himself, but was rejected. Instead, Pastor von Bodelschwingh was elected, a man of genuinely Evangelical theology and life, the head of the establishment at Bethel-bei-Bielefeld. At this the German Christians stirred up agitation within the Church and to restore order the government appointed a commissioner over Church affairs. Bodelschwingh resigned.

Already there had been protests from many quarters in the Church. As early as January a group meeting at Altona, the parish of Hans Asmussen, a contributor to *Zwischen den Zeiten*, had declared that the Church must carry on its task of serving Christ and his Gospel in freedom from outside pressure. Again, the call by the German Christian Congress in April 1933 for the unification of the Church had been answered by Otto Dibelius, General Superintendent of the church in Brandenburg, in a pastoral letter: 'We are united in affirming that the Gospel stands in opposition to all human ideology, whether nationalist or socialist, liberal or conservative. The Gospel must not be subservient to the selfish wishes of men but must be their judge' (quoted in A. S. Duncan Jones: *Struggle for Religious Freedom in Germany*, p. 36).

But from the professor at Bonn had come no independent statement. In 1932 had appeared Volume I, Part 1 of the *Church*

Dogmatics. No doubt he was, in the midst of these unhappy events, proceeding with Volume I, Part 2, and with the teaching of his many pupils. And yet it was characteristic neither of the man nor of his theology that he should have nothing to say to this situation.

His word, when it came, was completely consistent, completely unexpected. On St John the Baptist's Day, June 24, 1933, Jäger was appointed Commissioner over the Prussian Churches. That evening Barth began a pamphlet which he finished the next day, a Sunday (thirteen thousand words in a day!). The title, no less unexpected but consistent, *Theologische Existenz heute!* — *Theological Existence Today!* Who can take exception to its being an uneven piece of writing? It has a passion and single-mindedness for the welfare of the Church that reminds us of the first of *Tracts for the Times*:

> To us no concern can be more pressing, no hope more moving than the concern and hope of our ministry. No friend can be dearer than one who helps us in this ministry, no foe more hateful than he who wants to hinder us in this ministry (p. 13).

> I maintain that this teaching is alien with no right to a place in the Evangelical Church. I maintain that it would be the end of the Evangelical Church if this teaching ever came to have sole sway within her, as the "German Christians" intend that it shall. I maintain that the Evangelical Church ought rather to become a tiny group and go into the catacombs than sign a peace, even covertly, with this doctrine (p. 50).

> I have a request to make to my various theological friends also, who find themselves shifted into being in a position to say Yes! to this teaching, having been "doped" or tricked by some sophism. I ask them to take note from me, that I feel myself utterly and finally divided from them, save so far as, by a lucky inconsistency, there may be retained by them some yet solid core of what is christian, churchly and theological, alongside this heresy (pp. 50-51).

And the final words:

> Oh, that the German evangelical theologian may remain awake! Or, if he has gone to sleep, that today, today, he might awake again! (pp. 84-85).

Why has Barth hitherto kept silence, when so many others have already confessed their faith and denied error? Why does he say: 'I endeavour to carry on theology, and only theology, now as previously, as if nothing had happened. Perhaps there is a slightly increased tone, but without direct allusions. It is something like the chanting of the hours by the Benedictines nearby in the *Maria Laach* which without any doubt continues the even tenor of its way, without break or interruption, even in the Third Reich' (p. 9). And now, instead of a stirring protest with some such title as *No Other Gods*, or even *The Threat to the Church's Existence*, this *Theological Existence Today!* makes its appearance, not speaking directly to the concrete situation but 'considering and working out the presuppositions needed every day' for speaking to the meaning of the situation.

The presuppositions are not political, whether secular or ecclesiastical. They are theological. And theological means precisely the same in *Theological Existence Today!* as it did in *Anselm: Fides Quaerens Intellectum*. We have said that two of the great works that flowed from the Anselm book were the *Church Dogmatics* and the theological foundation of the German Confessing Church. In the one, Barth strove to write a Dogmatics that was a theology of the Word alone; in the other, he strove to impress on all Christians the need for the Church to be built on and to live by the Word alone. Just as theology cannot be founded on a philosophy, since faith and understanding are created and determined by their object, so the Church must not take her stand on anything but the Word of God which has called her into being and which supplies her life. She has no other task but to proclaim God's Word — the Word who was crucified, dead, buried, raised again the third day, and sits at the right hand of the Father. This Word has triumphed over us and all its other enemies, and therefore it will triumph now and always. It is only in his Word, who is Jesus Christ, found in the Scriptures, that God is our God. If we do not believe this, we are not members of the Church.

Theologians are called to be ministers of the Word. They may neglect their calling. They may omit to pray for understanding. They may forget the exclusiveness of the Word and try to help God's Word with all sorts of human aids, trying to face and solve problems by other means. 'By doing this, we show that we do not esteem God to be a working factor in anything as

Creator, Reconciler, and Redeemer. That our hearts are thus divided between God's Word and all other sorts of things which, avowedly or tacitly, we invest with Divine glory' (p. 15). There is nothing wrong in being a secular or church politician. But this is not the same as being a theologian; and theologians are called to be theologians, to lead a theological existence.

The rest of the book is a statement of the meaning of the events in Germany up to midsummer 1933 in the light of these theological presuppositions. Church reform by the state; the new order of bishops; the German Christian Movement and its doctrines; the committee of three appointed in May; the opposition by the so-called "New Reformation" group — all these are subjected to theological examination, are considered as constituting situations in which it is necessary for theologians simply to be genuine theologians, the Church only to be the Church.

By refusing to be anything but a theologian, by binding the faith and activity of the Church to their object, Barth spoke a word that laid bare the significance of the incipient struggle. He himself later wrote that 'as a matter of fact, the situation in Germany is extraordinarily simple. Just here, in all important questions, it is possible to answer with a plain Yes or No' (*Introduction* to A. Frey: *Cross and Swastika*, p. 11). It was he, however, who in these early months exposed the true meaning of what was happening, by stripping away the irrelevancies and sophistries that obscured the issue. How eagerly his word was seized upon is shown by the great sale of *Theological Existence Today!* My own German copy bears the date 1933 (I do not know if it was part of the last edition in that year) and already it is the eighth impression, comprising the 25th-28th thousand copies.

This pamphlet started a new periodical (which is still running) with the same title of *Theologische Existenz heute*. It was edited by Barth and Thurneysen and appeared monthly from October 1933. Of the first twenty numbers twelve were written by Barth, and the rest by Ernst Wolf, Thurneysen, Heinrich Vogel, Asmussen, Peter Barth and Edmund Schlink. The Forewords to those by Barth contain much information and comment on the Church conflict and are to be found in Karl Barth: *The German Church Conflict*. The seventh number, in February 1934, coincided with the last number of *Zwischen den Zeiten*, started with enthusiasm twelve years before as the organ of "Dialectic Theology", but now doomed as the leaders found that their supposed common point-of-view was breaking into irreconcilable fragments. 'In the ten years following the World War my friends and I had found each other in common thought and intentions in terms of certain oppositions we held in common and in terms of certain general positions. We believed that we might give, one to the other, mutual confidence and support. But as the sun went up — and this is what happened in the decade we are looking back on now — those of these fellowships which had not really been fellow-ships at all were dissolved like the morning mist. I know now that it had to be that Friedrich Gogarten should develop into a sinister-looking new German state theologian. It had to be that Georg Merz should work out his own salvation in a half-patriar-chal half-pastoral combination, with a bit of Luther, a bit of Hitler, and a bit of Blumhardt. It had to be that Emil Brunner should turn to a new apologetic of his own invention, and should at the same time throw himself into the arms of the Buchman Group movement' (*How I Changed*, pp. 41-2).

From the end of the summer, when Müller had become *Reichsbischof* in place of Bodelschwingh, the opponents of the German Christians were subjected to great pressure. The General Synod of the Prussian Church on September 5 voted for the de-privation of ministers who were suspect politically as well as of those who had even a Jewish grandparent. Talk of concentration camps was already in the air. But the opposition was gathering strength and assurance, and a "Gospel and Church" group came into existence, refusing to take part in the bogus election by which Müller was made *Reichsbischof*, and attacking the new régime as in fact illegal, in that it contravened Article 1 of the Church Con-stitution which the state itself had accepted: 'The unshakeable foundation of the German Evangelical Church is the Gospel of Jesus Christ, as it is revealed to us in the Holy Scriptures and has come anew to light in the confessions of the Reformation.' In October Martin Niemöller, Pastor of the Berlin church of Dahlem, drafted the terms of the newly formed Pastors' Emer-gency League — terms which sprang from *Theological Existence*

Today! — the first of which ran: 'I engage to execute my office as Minister of the Word, holding myself bound to the Holy Scriptures and to the Confessions of the Reformation as the true exegesis of the Holy Scriptures.' Niemöller was a dangerous enemy. He was not a nobody who could be silenced summarily. His record as a naval officer in the Great War, his unimpeachable patriotism, combined with his quick recognition of a spade as a spade and his uninhibited declaration that it was a spade, made him an excellent advocate of a theology that demanded the virtues of a clear sight, a single mind, and courage.

In this month also Barth refused an invitation to make one of the members of the theological committee in the constitution of the state church and at the same time resigned from the examining board in the Rhine Consistory. These actions he took on the ground that, although the opportunities for having a voice in affairs might seem useful, his continued participation would imply recognition of an heretical usurpation.

The notorious meeting at the *Sportpalast* in Berlin on November 13, presided over by Hossenfelder, and treated to a gross and foolish attack on the Jewish Old Testament and the Jewish Rabbi Paul by one Krause, was answered by a proclamation from the pulpits of members of the Pastors' Emergency League recognising the whole Bible as the Word of God valid for faith and life. This meeting probably did more good than harm, for it showed up the German Christians in their true light and consequently divided the spirits more definitely. It also stirred up considerable agitation in the Church, as a result of which Müller was forced to dismiss Hossenfelder.

But Barth was not happy about the attitude of the opposition: 'When I attended the meeting of the leaders of the Pastors' Emergency league, I found it moved and concerned more passionately over the possibility of an ecclesiastical and political exploitation of the situation created by the scandal of the Sportspalace . . . and less passionately over the fundamental reflection demanded on that important day than behoves the good management of the Church's opposition today' (*German Church Conflict*, p. 19). The opposition must understand that nothing had been changed. The Krause speech was merely a wild expression of

German Christian teaching. The fact that he had been disowned in no way represented a change in that teaching. The point at issue, Barth insisted once again, is a conflict between the Church and a particular form of neo-Protestantism. If the indignation roused by Krause's "crude paganism" had been expended on the initial victories of the German Christians in the summer, good might have resulted. Nor should the opposition now be too cock-a-hoop at the dismissal of Hossenfelder and the secessions from the German Christian ranks. 'What is in store for us could be worse than what has already happened' (*German Church Conflict*, p. 25).

The year 1934 opened with the first of two synods to be held at Wuppertal-Barmen in Westphalia. This first one was addressed by Barth on the meaning of the Reformed Confessions of the German Church and passed a declaration declaring the freedom of the Church in its service of the Gospel. This declaration is also noteworthy for its uniting of Lutherans and Reformed in a common confession. The nineteenth century Church Union in Prussia had been based rather on a neglect of confession; the Nazi unification had been political — indeed, the present situation is the last phase of the old Union, wrote Barth. But there is possible a genuine uniting in a common confession, and 'I think I have said everything [in the Declaration of Barmen 1] in such a way that stalwart Lutherans, without on their part sacrificing anything, could speak with us [Reformed] .... I believe that in this way and no other can one and *must* one confess in the German Evangelical Church today. Lutherans and Reformed cannot and must not confess today in opposition, but rather in unison as evangelical-Lutherans and evangelical-Reformed' (*German Church Conflict*, pp. 26-7). It looked now as if the opposition was winning. At the famous meeting on January 25 between the German Christians and the opposition, at which Hitler himself was present, they even felt sufficiently in control to offer terms — that Müller should go on extended leave and his place be taken by one of themselves, Bishop Marahrens of Hanover. There followed the dramatic intervention of Goering, revealing an indiscretion of Niemöller's (learned by tapping his telephone) to the effect that Hitler was about to be dismissed.

The fat was in the fire now. The Bishops present speedily dis-
sociated themselves from any suspicion of any sort of disrespect
towards the head of the state, far less of being guilty of wanting
his removal. Müller and his German Christians were once again
firmly in the saddle.

In April, however, at a conference in Ulm, the opposition,
now becoming known as *Die bekennende Kirche*, the Confessing
Church, tacitly claimed to be the true Evangelical Church in
Germany. This claim it did not again surrender.

The first Synod of Barmen had been attended mainly by
representatives from the western parts of Germany. The second
was the Confessional Synod of the whole German Evangelical
Church. This is the famous Synod of Barmen, held in the Markt-
kirche from May 29-31, 1934. Its Declaration, framed by Barth
and presented by Hans Asmussen, must rank with the famous
Protestant Confessions of Faith. Indeed, Barth himself pointed
out that this was the first time in the history of the Church that
the Church had explicitly denied natural theology. For the first
and basic article runs:

> "I am the way, the truth, and the life. No man cometh unto
> the Father but by me" (John 14.6).
> "Verily, verily, I say unto you, He that entereth not by the
> door into the sheepfold, but climbeth up some other way, the
> same is a thief and a robber. I am the door: by me if any man
> enter in, he shall be saved" (John 10.1,9).
> Jesus Christ, as he is testified to us in Holy Scripture, is the
> one Word of God which we have to hear and which we have to
> trust and obey in life and in death.
> *We reject the false doctrine* that the church may and must
> acknowledge as sources of its proclamation other events, powers,
> forms and truths as God's revelation beside this one Word of God.

This was, said Barth in *Church Dogmatics* II, 1, a declaration which went far beyond the immediate situation in Germany.
It contained a purifying from natural theology for the whole
Church. As Asmussen said, it was directed 'against the phenomenon which for more than two hundred years had slowly prepared
the devastation of the church'. But in its immediate context it
was directed against the theology of Schleiermacher and Ritschl.
It is, therefore, the confessional counterpart to *The Epistle to*

the Romans and the *Church Dogmatics*. And once again it must be said that neither *Theological Existence Today!* nor the Barmen Declaration represented anything new in Barth's thought. They were restating, in a new situation, an already held point of view. The thinking that made possible his stand in the German Church conflict had been done eighteen months before, for *Anselm: Fides Quaerens Intellectum*. Had he not learnt then how to base theology upon its own object, so making it unnecessary and therefore pernicious to seek other foundations, he would not now have been able to show how the Church must renounce all other ways of living and acting save that of faith in the Incarnate Word witnessed in the Scriptures. The confessional basis of the Confessing Church was Christological in a way that had hardly been known since the days of the simple confession of the earliest Church: "I believe in the Lord Jesus Christ". The Confessing Church was a society that took its stand on Jesus Christ as the unique and complete revelation of God.

The following October the Confessing Church formed an Executive Council for itself, composed of a President, Koch, a Theological Adviser, Asmussen, a Lutheran and a Calvinist Representative, Meiser and Barth respectively, and a Union Representative, Martin Niemöller. Now this did mean a change for Barth. He had maintained hitherto a purely theological position. The theology at this point had to assume a political character. This is not to say that theology was replaced by politics, theological reasoning by political and pragmatic motivations, but that the theology had to be applied to certain concrete situations and considerations. It goes without saying that the policies concerned were properly those of the Church; if they were also state policies, this was not because the Confessing Church wished to meddle in state affairs but because the state had refused to recognize the Church as a separate entity from itself.

Barth's days of active participation in the affairs of the Confessing Church were numbered, however. The government which had thought good to destroy the liberty of the Church and the conscience of mankind, now expelled professors of philosophy and drove learning into exile, that nothing honourable might offend the guilty state. A new law demanding from all university teachers a personal oath of allegiance to Hitler was invoked against Barth, and, since he would only take it with the proviso: 'so far as I can as an evangelical Christian', he was prosecuted. He also refused to begin his lectures by giving the Nazi salute: "Heil, Hitler!" His lectures commenced with prayer. In November 1934 he was suspended by the Rector of the University and in the following month the Local Officials' Disciplinary Court at Cologne ordered his dismissal. 'Nearly thirty years ago now,' he told the inmates of Basel prison in 1963, 'in the days of Hitler, in Cologne on the Rhine, I too once appeared in court. I was there accused and charged by a wicked lawyer who said that I had done what was not allowed in the Germany of the day and had not done what ought to be done in the Germany of the day. Three judges sat opposite me and looked at me with serious, suspicious faces. And an able young lawyer [Otto Bleibtrau, later Secretary of State in the North Rhine Westphalian Ministry of Justice] sat beside me and took great pains to prove that everything was not as bad as all that. Everything took its inevitable course. I was found guilty and sentenced to be dismissed as an unreliable state official and as a bad teacher of German youth' (*Call For God*, p. 88).

On his appeal, the Prussian Administrative High Court quashed the sentence and ordered instead the relatively mild punishment of a fine consisting of a fifth of a year's salary. The Court was over-ridden by the Minister of Education, who upheld the sentence of dismissal. *The Times* of London (Tuesday, June 25, 1935) reported all this under the heading *Dr. Karl Barth Retired*, and devoted the second leader to his case as an example of inhumanity by a régime which nevertheless, as G. M. Young had pointed out a little earlier, had done much for Germany. If the Nazis were not to forfeit all our sympathy, they must learn to behave like a civilized government.

The following year *The Times* had a rather more dramatic story to tell (Thursday, October 10, 1935), which it put under a misleadingly startling headline:

'DR. KARL BARTH ARRESTED IN GERMANY

Dr. Karl Barth, the distinguished Protestant theologian, has been arrested on German soil and expelled.

Dr. Barth has been living in Switzerland, of which he is a citizen, since his dismissal from the Chair of Evangelical Theology at Bonn University and the refusal by the authorities to allow him even to act as a private tutor on account of the part he played on the Confessional side in the German Church conflict. He came into Germany to deliver the principal address at an Evangelical Theological Week at Barmen, in the Ruhr, where the first Reich Synod of the Confessional Church met last year. He was arrested by the police and put back across the border to-day as an undesirable alien.   (Berlin, October 9).'

What Barth meant to the Confessing Church was voiced by Hans Asmussen: 'As I see it, his significance for the Confessing Church lay in that he, in its quiet origin before the disorder of the Church, in its visible work and also in evil and guilty days, went hand in hand with us as teacher of the Church, as pastor of souls, bishop and brother, neither overwhelming us nor failing for friendship's sake to check us, so that he might call us with the binding and loosing Words of the Lord himself.'

In the midst of the German Church struggle there occurred the most dramatic theological controversy of our age. It will be remembered that Eduard Thurneysen had voiced doubts about Emil Brunner away back in 1924. But they seem not to have been doubts shared by Barth at this time. It was not until "after 1929" that Brunner's course began to give him concern. Brunner's two great works, *The Mediator* and *The Divine Imperative,* were published in 1927 and 1932. Even in *The Mediator* the post-1930 Barth must have found many things which violated his understanding of the nature of theology. In *Church Dogmatics* I,1 (Summer 1932) Barth had already written very sharply against Brunner's playing off of apologetics against dogmatics, of asking *whether* God exists (see pp. 27-32). In October 1932 he makes it clear that he does not wish his name to be coupled with Brunner's: 'May I also ask my English readers . . . not to look at me simply through the spectacles of Emil Brunner, not to conform me to his pattern' (*The Author's Preface to the English Edition, The Epistle to the Romans,* p. vii).

Brunner was urged to retaliate. He at first refused, saying that, although he obviously did not like Barth's attacks, he so much approved of his theology in general and even of his intention in the attacks, that he was willing to put up with the misunderstanding. Barth, he said wittily, was a soldier on sentry duty at night who 'from time to time also annihilates a good friend whose password he does not hear or misunderstands in his eagerness' (*Natural Theology*, p. 16). So far as he himself was concerned, Barth had missed; but he could not be angry with him, for the shot was not fired in enmity. He would not therefore retaliate, but would only make three points: (1) his intention is no different from Barth's; (2) but Barth draws the wrong conclusions from the right intention; and (3) Barth is therefore wrong to accuse him of betraying their common intention.

The working out of these theses is the substance of the booklet *Nature and Grace* (1934). There have been efforts made to form a theology apart from God's self-revelation in Jesus Christ. The foundation and the existence of such theology have been man's self-knowledge, and his knowledge of the universe and of events, whether historical or personal. This is called natural theology. It is unchristian and was completely abhorrent to such a Biblical theologian as Brunner. The theme of *Nature and Grace*, however, is that there is a Christian natural theology, that is to say, one which exists in relationship to Jesus Christ. It is partly a preparation for the Gospel, an apologetics which is able to speak to men on the basis of what they cannot truthfully deny, in order to lead on then to the meaning of it all, Jesus Christ, Saviour and Lord. It is partly also a subsidiary aid for the believer. The believer finds and knows the God who reveals himself in Jesus Christ in the Scriptures and in the universe which he has created, in his continual activity in history. This Christian natural theology, says Brunner, is taught by the Bible and the Reformers and is perfectly consistent with Barth's own theology. In face of the terrible danger based on a false natural theology now threatening the Church (he means, of course, the German Christian heresy), 'It is the task of our theological generation to find the way back to a true *theologia naturalis*' (*Natural Theology*, p. 59).

The November 1934 number of *Theologische Existenz heute* was *Nein! Antwort an Emil Brunner — No! Answer to Emil*

Brunner. The rejection was total, from the *Angry Introduction* to the counterblast of the final sentences: 'Only the church and the theology of the antichrist can profit from [natural theology]. The Evangelical Church and Evangelical theology would only sicken and die of it' (*Natural Theology*, p. 128). Barth denied that the Bible taught a Christian natural theology or that Luther and Calvin had made it a theological aim. (The scientific refutation of Brunner's interpretation of Luther and Calvin was committed to Ernst Wolf and Peter Barth — their essays appeared as numbers 6 and 18 of *Theologische Existenz heute*). He denied also that he had himself considered the pursuit of natural theology to be part of the theological programme. 'Ever since about 1916, when I began to recover noticeably from the effects of my theological studies and the influences of the liberal-political pre-war theology, my opinion concerning the task of our theological generation has been this: we must learn again to understand revelation as *grace* and grace as *revelation* and therefore turn away from all "true" or "false" *theologia naturalis* by ever making new decisions and being ever converted anew' (*Natural Theology*, p. 71).

The burden of *Nein!* is: Jesus Christ is the complete self-revelation of God; how then can there be any need, let alone any place, for some other source of knowledge of God? St Paul and, depending upon him, Luther and Calvin, had taught the unrealized possibility of knowledge through creation, and had taught it purely within the context of God's judgment and man's inexcusability. They had not made it a positive preparation for faith in Christ. A programme of apologetics as a preliminary to the Gospel was therefore ruled out. The good news about Jesus Christ creates its own point of contact between God and the hearer. Brunner's Christian natural theology, however, demanded an already existing relationship between God and man, that man was not "dead in trespasses and sins", but had a certain link with God. For this reason, Barth said, Brunner stands fundamentally in the same position as the neo-Protestants and the Roman Catholics. In a savagely satirical passage he imagines himself seeking, if not an audience of the Pope, at any rate an interview with one of the Vatican theologians (he was writing

the pamphlet in Rome) and explaining that Protestants had misunderstood the Reformation; that in fact Brunner had shown
that Luther and Calvin held the heart of the Romanist theology,
man was only wounded, not dead: 'You are amazed, my good
Roman Catholic friend! Perhaps you have a suspicion that these
might merely be the views of some neo-Protestant and therefore not to be considered binding, while the main force of Protestantism, supported by the Reformers themselves, might stand
in quite a different place? But abandon your suspicions. Understand that — quite apart from the authority of Brunner — what
I have been telling you is in the main nothing but the genuine
teaching of the fierce and terrible Calvin, whom you would
hardly have suspected of such a thing and from whom "we" had
merely failed to enquire soon enough. But now we have en-
quired! Read Brunner's 126 quotations from Calvin and look
forward to the as yet unpublished work of his pupil, G. Gloede,
in which you will find an absolutely "enormous number of references" of the same kind' (*Natural Theology*, pp. 98-99).

Barth is so angry, so positive, because it was Brunner who
had written *Nature and Grace* and because he had written it
in 1934. Had the book come from Hirsch or even from one of
the better-class German Christians, it would not have been so
bad. But Brunner was in the public mind associated with Barth
and all that he stood for. Barth was determined that there should
be no excuse for anyone to be ignorant of his theological position. And — 1934! Could there have been chosen a more un-
fortunate, more inept time to publish such a work? The German
Christians were quick to recognize a theological ally, a softening
of the hard line of Barmen, and gave a welcome to *Nature and
Grace*.

Friendly relations, personal as well as theological, were
henceforth severed between Barth and Brunner. Barth steadily
pursued his way. Brunner went on to write *Revelation and Reason* and a three-volume *Dogmatics*. Apparently a personal reconciliation between the two was engineered by an American
student in 1960; an unnecessary and sentimental piece of ecu-
menism. Had they ever been close comrades?

At this time also Barth began to lecture in various parts of

Europe on the ancient Creeds and the Reformation Confessions of Faith. The theological reason for this choice of subject was his ever stronger awareness of the continuity of the Church and its theology. 'There manifestly exists for me what might be called an authoritativeness in Early Church doctrine' (*Church Dogmatics*, I,1, p. X). The historical reason lay in the situation of the Church in Germany. The struggling Church was being urged to stand fast by its old confessions, the Augsburg of 1530, the Heidelberg Catechism of 1563 and so on. Hans Asmussen wrote a brochure for *Theologische Existenz heute* (No. 16) on 'The Church of the Augsburg Confession' (1934). Barth himself contributed, as Number 29, 'The Confession of the Reformation and our Confession' (1935). What was happening to the German Church, however, was a danger ever present to every Church. The Church is always threatened by the temptation to give its allegiance to other powers besides Jesus Christ its Lord. Therefore Barth never tired of proclaiming to Churches the meaning of the early Church creeds and of their own confessions. When he was asked in later years if he would consider writing a book on the *Thirty-nine Articles of Religion* he regretted that he was too old to start on a new study, for he would have liked, he said, to remind the Church of England what her Articles meant.

The first of these sets of lectures was on the Apostles' Creed and was given at the University of Utrecht in February and March 1935. The signs of the great conflict lie everywhere in them. When they are published as *Credo*, they bear the noble dedication:

1935!

TO THE MINISTERS
HANS ASMUSSEN
HERMANN HESSE
KARL IMMER
MARTIN NIEMÖLLER
HEINRICH VOGEL
IN MEMORY OF ALL WHO
STOOD
STAND
AND WILL STAND

At the back of Barth's mind in this book there is always the fight of the Confessing Church against heresy — not simply its immediate manifestation, the heresy of the German Christians, not even the heresy of "neo-Protestantism", but the fundamental heresy of I John 4.3: "every spirit which does not confess Jesus is not of God". In the midst of his exposition of the clause "and in Jesus Christ, his only Son, our Lord" he will say: 'It can be asserted and proved with the utmost definiteness and accuracy that the great theological-ecclesiastical catastrophe of which the German Protestantism of the moment is the arena, would have been impossible if the three words *Filium eius unicum* in the properly understood sense of the Nicene trinitarian doctrine had not for more than two hundred years been really lost to the German Church amongst a chaos of reinterpretations designed to make them innocuous. This catastrophe should be a real, final warning to the evangelical churches, and especially to the theological faculties of other lands, where, so far as trinitarian dogma is concerned, no better ways are being trodden' (p. 49).

CHAPTER SEVEN

The Church Dogmatics

BARTH LEFT GERMANY AT THE END OF 1934 AND LIVED IN SWIT-
zerland for the next few months, pending the fate of his appeal.
When in mid-June 1935 the German Minister of Education had
settled the matter, the university of his native and ancestral city,
Basel, at once created for him a Chair of Systematic Theology.
Here he remained for the rest of his life; and it was from here
that the many volumes of the *Church Dogmatics* came forth.

The first had been published while he was still at Bonn in
1932. This was the complete rewriting of the abortive attempt
of 1927. Now even the title is changed. No longer *Christian
Dogmatics*, for Christian as a word has been suspect since Kierkegaard's attacks on "Christendom", and we may well question the
wisdom of Barth's using it in the first place. It has become *Church
Dogmatics*. Theology does not take place merely within Christendom, but within the sphere of the Church, and what is more,
of the particular church of the theologian. No theologian can be
a general "Christian" theologian; he must be a Reformed or a
Roman Catholic or an Anglican theologian. The word *Church*
also reflects Barth's awareness that he was working in the line of
a long tradition.

The chief lines of the book have not changed. It is still
Prolegomena to Dogmatics, it is still *The Doctrine of the Word
of God*. But what he said then Barth has now reconsidered in
the light of his new understanding of theological method. This
demands clarification. For what does "theological method" mean
for a theologian? How does he construct his theology by means
of a method?

Let us refresh our minds with a glance back at *Anselm:
Fides Quaerens Intellectum*. We summarized Barth's method as
comprising four facets. The first facet of the method of theology
is that it is turned towards God as its object. The second facet

is that it is turned towards Jesus Christ. The third is that it is
turned towards the witness of the Scriptures to Jesus Christ. The
fourth is that both faith and the understanding which starts
from it and which is all the time motivated by it, are determined
by their object and correspond to it. How does the theologian
employ his method in practice?

In the first place, it does not mean that the method is a
central principle from which he can construct each doctrine as he
comes to it. This is a course which, I suspect, is fathered on
systematic theologians by the critics and which would prove un-
workable in practice. Some nineteenth century (and even today
some old-fashioned) Calvin scholars, for example, would describe
Calvin's method as an outworking of one central theme — predestination and the sovereignty of God were favourite choices.
There is a danger lest Barth should be treated in the same way,
and his method viewed so statically that he is conceived of as
trying to understand everything in terms of a principle called
"the Word of God", or "Christology", or "triumphant grace",
or "faith seeking understanding". All this is abstract thinking,
thinking which may start from an understanding gained from
Scripture but which then continues on its own free way. It is a
course of thinking which is not controlled throughout by its
object — the Church's confession in Scripture — but by its own
starting-point. What is bound to happen in the event is that when
Scripture is appealed to, it is made to fit into the meaning of
the principle and is not allowed freedom to speak. It would be
hard to deny that there are places in the *Church Dogmatics*
where Barth fails to prevent this happening. That it is not his
intention that it should ever happen, however, is abundantly
clear.

What theological method means in practice is the study of
and meditation on the Scriptures as the witness to God's self-
revelation in Jesus Christ. It is an activity of faith and therefore
of prayer for the understanding of Jesus Christ in Scripture; not
Simon Magus prayer, that wants understanding so that a good
dogmatics may be written, but David prayer, that longs for the
knowledge of God "like as the hart desireth the water-brooks".
The study of Scripture involves the various well-known disci-

plines — a knowledge of languages, of social and political history, and so on. With the use of these as tools, and not as ends in themselves, there must be a careful attention to what the Bible is saying. There is no *mystique* about this; it is the requisite for the understanding of any document whatsoever. We shall never understand a piece of literature just by skimming it through. With the Bible, however, this careful attention is more than an endeavour to understand the author; it is an act of obedience to the declaration of God's will. The theologian, moreover, is not the first man who ever read the Bible. Around him are scores or hundreds of people using their particular talents to shed light on it: Old Testament scholars, New Testament scholars, linguists, historians, fellow theologians. Behind him, stretching back over two thousand years, are the exegetes and dogmatic theologians of the Church. Sometimes for better, sometimes for worse, the witness of the Bible has been understood in certain ways or forms, and these forms have been arranged, now in this, now in that, order. In other words, from relatively early times, the teaching of the Bible has been systematized in doctrines: the "doctrine" of the Trinity; the "doctrine" of grace; the "doctrine" of man; the "doctrine" of reconciliation. Or we can say the word "dogma" for "doctrine". It would be abstract thinking to try to construct dogmatics as if this had not happened or to start afresh without the dogmas of the past. Not that the dogmas must be treated as equally authoritative with the Bible. They, too, must be criticised and, if necessary, corrected to bring them into line with the witness of the Scriptures.

This was the aim and method that Barth proposed to himself in writing the *Church Dogmatics*. Because it is the understanding of the Biblical witness to Christ, he excises the apparent attempt made in the first edition to understand faith in Christ by way of existentialism. It is the voice of Scripture to which he listens throughout and by which he lets his thinking be guided.

To halt the progress of Protestant dogmatics and set it on a new course will not be achieved either by prophetic utterances, however inspired, or by run-of-the-mill dogmatics that says nothing very much. For two hundred years, Barth believed, Protestant theology had been going drastically astray. Some might believe that the remedy would lie in repeating the theology previous to the straying, that is, broadly speaking, the theology of the Reformation. Not so Barth. For one thing, he believed that the mere repetition of an old theology in modern terms, however good it was in its own day and however much it might have to teach us, results in an unreal theology. Each age must bear its own theological witness to Christ, and that means bearing witness in its own way. Moreover, the theology of the Reformation was not only ignorant of the many problems that have emerged since the sixteenth century, but was also not impeccable in itself. If repetition is not allowed, the task becomes formidable. If it is to have any success at all, it must be carried out thoroughly, in such a way that the great error of the past is put right and that what is written does not give fresh occasion to that error, perhaps in another form, or a similar error.

This is one reason for the vast size of the *Church Dogmatics,* for which Barth has been often castigated. The words have been counted, the time spent on writing it, on reading it, deplored. Such quantity surveying is theological Philistinism. I have never seen a golden eagle in the wild, but if I did, I should not try to count its feathers. *The Christian Dogmatics* of 1927 was a mere four hundred pages or so. To say all that he thought necessary, and to say it in the way that he thought necessary, demanded more than four times that size. Such a book would have made a nice folio in the old days, but this was judged unsuitable for the twentieth century and the work was therefore issued in two parts, of which the second did not appear until 1938. 'Yes, for a right understanding and exposition there is need of a thorough elucidation. May it not be that I have been too short and not too long at some important points?' (II,2, p. ix).

The compass of the whole work he foresaw and determined at the outset. There would be, he says in the Foreword to I,1, a second half-volume of pretty much the same size, completing the Prolegomena, the doctrine of Revelation. The second volume would contain the doctrine of God, the third the doctrine of Creation, the fourth the doctrine of Reconciliation, the fifth the doctrine of Redemption.

The initial prospectus has been closely followed in general:

the doctrines of Revelation, God, Creation, and Reconciliation. But the path led into some unexpected places, unexpected even to the author himself. 'When I take up the theme of each part-volume, or even embark upon each new section, although I keep to a general direction, only the angels in heaven do actually know in detail what form the material will take . . . . as far as I am concerned it is enough if I am clear that at each point I listen as unreservedly as possible to the witness of Scripture and as impartially as possible to that of the Church, and then consider and formulate whatever may be the result' (IV,2, pp. x-xi).

The manner of composition was the same for very many years, although I do not know if it obtained from the beginning. The substance of the volumes was originally prepared as his university lectures. It was written out in long-hand, in his tiny, crabbed writing. This was typed by his secretary to serve as the lectures. After the lectures came the serious work of revision in preparation for publication, and here he received inestimable help from Fräulein Charlotte von Kirschbaum, a most gifted woman. She had been with Barth since 1930, and, it is said, learned Hebrew and Greek in order to be of the greater use.

The work is arranged in distinctive style, a style that he had not before employed; even the 1927 *Christian Dogmatics* was cast in a conventional mould. Now we are confronted with passages in large print and passages in small print. Those in large print are the dogmatic reasoning, and rarely contain any quotations except from the Bible. Those in small print, otherwise called excursuses or excursūs (either of which seems to be the accepted plural of this less than lovely word *excursus*), contain what Barth calls 'biblical and theological presuppositions, the connections with the history of theology and the polemical relations of my statements' (I,1, p. VIII). In other words, in these excursūs are set out the quotations (in full) from the Bible and from other sources and the critique of the theology of past and present. Barth took care to arrange it so that the large print passages would read as a connected whole, and, indeed, says that the *Church Dogmatics* could, if necessary, be read through like that, with the excursūs omitted. One may doubt, however, whether the meaning would be fully understood, for the quotations are more than gilt on the gingerbread. They give a certain slant and interpretation to the argument. They show how Barth's thoughts have been running historically. Take an example from the very first page:

> Dogmatics is a theological discipline. And theology is a function of the Church.
>
> The Church confesses God by the fact that she speaks of God. She does so first of all through her existence in the activity of each individual believer. And she does so in the second place through her special activity as a community.

The excursus which follows this paragraph runs:

> Theology is *the reason or word concerning the divinity* (Augustine: *The City of God,* VIII, 1). *Theology is speaking of God, from God, before God, to his glory (Cocceius: Summa theol.* 1669 I,1).

Now, without getting ourselves entangled in an historical discussion, we may take note of what is immediately obvious. Barth is able to call upon the great Church Father and the Protestant scholastic for support. This means that he is saying something which has been common knowledge in the Church for centuries. It is also at once clear that he is not simply repeating what they had said, but has thought about it in a fresh way and has introduced some different concepts — "Church", "confession", "confession to God consists not only of proclamation in preaching, but also of the Sacraments, worship, teaching, missionary work, the care of the sick and those in need". So we see that the excursus not only illuminates the reasoning but the reasoning also casts a light on the excursus and therefore is a running commentary on the history of doctrine. For this reason the reader should not treat the excursūs as if they were time-wasting hindrances, but should listen to the voices which Barth listened to and consider what he has said in the light of them.

Not all the excursūs recall us to classical theology, however. Some are distinctly less formal. In the section on *The Holy Day* (III,4), for instance: 'Is there anything more depressing than the sight of obviously very bored male and female humanity wandering about our streets about three o'clock on a Sunday all dressed up and pushing prams? What is the point of it? Do we not feel (and from the look of them they feel it even more

strongly) that we would like to see them voluntarily put back
to some sort of useful activity?' (p. 61). Or, an unexpected note
in such a work: 'I once had two experiences closely related in
time. The first was on a Saturday evening when I attended a
variety show which was perfect in all its items and therefore, so
far as I could see, executed with a real righteousness of works.
The second was on the following Sunday morning when I listened to an extremely poor sermon, a real piece of theological
bungling. Could I resist the impression that, formally at least,
the right thing had been done at the place of very secular amuse-
ment and not at the place where the Gospel is preached and worship offered?' (III,4, p. 529). Certainly not what we should look
to find in Aquinas, Calvin or the austere Turretini; but no less
certainly completely consistent with Barth's humane theology.

The excursūs contain incidentally a great wealth of Biblical
exegesis and of history of doctrines. The man who in 1924 was
bemoaning his lack of learning and his weak Latin has made
himself one of the most learned of all the great systematic theologians. Comparisons are odious, but it is difficult to think of a
creative systematic theologian who has been his superior, or even
his equal. The one or two who come to mind (Melanchthon,
for example, the preceptor of Germany) were very learned in
certain fields. But Barth never wrote on any subject of which he
had not first mastered the literature, whether it was an early
Christological controversy or the Augustinian doctrine of predestination or such problems as abortion, euthanasia, and contra-
ception; in the literature of theology, philosophy, the physical
sciences, history, he moves with ease.

Therefore also many of the excursūs are important essays in
their own right. We might think of the profound exposition of
Genesis I,1 — 2.3 in Volume III, 1 from about p. 99 to p. 228,
or the exposition of the Synod of Barmen (II,1, pp. 172ff.),
or the passage on hymns (I,2, pp. 252ff.), or that on Mariology
(I,2, pp. 139ff.), or those on angels, scattered through the final
section of Volume III,3, or the assessments of various books on
marriage, the family, war, capital punishment, and such subjects, in Volume III,4.

No doubt a book will one day be written on Barth's

"sources", which will examine all the citations he makes at every stage of his career. We can hardly undertake such a task now. But everyone who has read Barth at all widely will carry in his remembrance the names of Overbeck, Kierkegaard, Dostoevsky, Blumhardt, Grünewald, Calvin, Luther, Nietzsche, from the earlier writings. In the 1922 *Epistle to the Romans* it is Dostoevsky who is mentioned the most frequently, followed far behind by Kierkegaard. In the *Church Dogmatics* most of these names occupy but a tiny space, and many new names are prominent. Of course, the number of references to an author is no indication of his worth or use; the context should be considered, as well as the place he is given in that context. Here we can speak only very generally; but we will remember the caution.

Luther and Calvin are quoted most often. After them comes Augustine, and then, with far fewer references, Thomas Aquinas and Schleiermacher. Whether in agreement or in disagreement, Barth is working with these voices sounding in his ears most insistently of all, the voices of Augustinianism, of Thomism, of the Reformation, and of neo-Protestantism. What of the rest of the early Church, however, and of Protestant scholasticism? The Greek fathers meet us quite frequently — Irenaeus, Athanasius, Gregory of Nyssa, especially. John Damascene and Ignatius show up strongly in the first two half-volumes, but are heard little thereafter. For the rest, it is less the Latin fathers, apart from Tertullian who is strongly represented, than the Apostles' and Nicene Creeds which play a large part. Among the Protestant scholastics, there stand out the Reformed theologians Polanus, Cocceius, Wolleb and Turretini, the Lutherans John Gerhard and Quenstedt.

But now we must notice a significant trend. By and large, what we may call the professional theologians occur most frequently in the first two volumes. Luther, Calvin, Augustine, and Schleiermacher hold their own all through; but for the rest, from Volume III onwards we hear more of the modern writers and the philosophers, artists and scientists. This is not accounted for solely by the fact that Volume III treats of the creation.

Now, too, in 1945 first appears Mozart. Of all the relations to Barth, Mozart seems, on the popular assessment of his music, the most strange. If anyone were to compare the 1922 *Epistle to the Romans* to Beethoven's music, it would occasion no surprise. If the *Church Dogmatics* were to be compared with a Bach fugue, we should know what was meant and begin to think of architectonics. But Mozart! I believe that David Friedrich Strauss spoke of "the incomparable Mozart" long before Barth, and I know that Kierkegaard, in *Either/Or*, called Mozart the greatest of all musicians and *Don Giovanni* the greatest of his works. But Barth! Why is it that he could call Mozart "incomparable" quite literally, unique even in the eighteenth century? Why is it that he made Mozart's music a part of his preparation for writing the *Church Dogmatics*, so that his custom was to listen to Mozart on the gramophone before he took up his pen? Why is it that the only bitter and unkind words in all the *Church Dogmatics* are spoken in defence of Mozart? That the Dutch neo-Calvinists should attack him, Barth says he is willing to accept: 'But it is going too far that in their attacks, obviously to offend me the more, they so far forget themselves as to use unrepeatable terms in disparagement of W. A. Mozart. In so doing they have, of course, shown themselves to be men of stupid, cold, and stony hearts to whom we need not listen" (III, 4, p. xiii).

The late date of the references in the *Church Dogmatics* must not be interpreted to mean that only in the nineteen-forties did Barth 'discover' Mozart. Mozart and music had been synonymous for him from his early childhood: 'My first meeting with great music — when a boy of about five or six years — came when I first met Mozart. I still remember the time when my father struck a few bars from the *Magic Flute* on the piano ("O my Camino, what happiness . . . !"); I was deeply moved' (*Religion and Culture*, p. 61).

The first substantial reference to Mozart does not come until Barth's series of lectures on the history of Protestant theology in the nineteenth century. The original course, dealing with that century only, was given at Münster in 1929 and Bonn in 1930. (These lectures, somewhat revised, were published in 1934). But in the winter semester of 1932-3 and in the following summer semester, they were expanded to take in the eighteenth century as the pre-history of the nineteenth; they were intended to go as far as Troeltsch, but in fact ceased at Ritschl. This course was not published until 1947 (1959 in English in an abbreviated form as *From Rousseau to Ritschl*). Their theme is the development of thought through the eighteenth century, leading to the Romantic movement towards the end of this century and the beginning of the next, and the course of theology which mirrored these movements as shown in the two outstanding theologians, Schleiermacher and Ritschl, and their satellites.

The great musical exponent of the Romantic movement was Beethoven, who is supposed to have explained his work by such outpourings as: 'I am the Bacchus who presses out for men this glorious wine and intoxicates their souls'; and 'what the spirit feels from music through the senses is the incarnation of spiritual perception'; and 'Every genuine creation of art is independent, mightier than the artist himself, and, through its manifestation, returns to the divine. With man it has only this in common, that it bears testimony to the mediation of the divine in him.' It is of such a conception that Barth writes: 'Music which holds the universe in thrall, which reflects ideas in the form of feeling, which aims at expressing and awakening the passions, which as feeling for life addresses itself in a mysterious way to the feeling for life, music which does not wish to be understood as beautiful, but as enchanting and only in a delirium . . . all that might very well be found in Schleiermacher's *Addresses on Religion*' (*From Rousseau to Ritschl*, p. 62). This, then, is the musical expression of the theology and world-view which Barth called neo-Protestantism and from which he was striving to free the Churches.

But there was another music of the eighteenth century which expressed quite a different conception of God and his world, which did not go into rhapsodies about the divinity of man, but knew that the divinity was in heaven and man on earth, which did not pour out its soul on to paper but expressed objectively its understanding of things. The best-known exponents of this music are Bach, Handel, Haydn and, supremely, Mozart. 'There was one musician who had all the things which distinguished the musicians of the eighteenth century from all those

who had gone before and from all those who came after, but
who had in addition something entirely personal to himself:
the sadness or horror inherent in the knowledge of the frontier
before which absolutist man, even and particularly when cutting
his finest figure, stands in blissful unawareness' (*From Rousseau
to Ritschl*, p. 51).

In *Church Dogmatics* III,3 Barth takes up and expands
this theme: 'Why is it that this man is so incomparable? Why is
it that for the receptive, he has produced in almost every bar
he conceived and composed a type of music for which "beautiful" is not a fitting epithet: music which for the true Christian
is not mere entertainment, enjoyment or edification but food
and drink; music full of comfort and counsel for his needs;
music which is never a slave to its techniques nor sentimental
but always "moving", free and liberating because wise, strong
and sovereign . . . . He had heard, and causes those who have ears
to hear, even today, what we shall not see until the end of time
— the whole context of providence. As though in the light of
this end, he heard the harmony of creation to which the shadow
also belongs but in which the shadow is not darkness, deficiency
is not defeat, sadness cannot become despair, trouble cannot de-
generate into tragedy and infinite melancholy is not ultimately
forced to claim undisputed sway. Thus the cheerfulness in this
harmony is not without its limits. But the light shines all the
more brightly because it breaks forth from the shadow . . . . He
heard the negative only in and with the positive. Yet in their in-
equality he heard them both together, as for example in the
Symphony in G minor of 1788 . . . . He died in misery like "an
unknown soldier" and in company with Calvin, and Moses in
the Bible, he has no known grave. But what does this matter?
What does a grave matter when a life is permitted simply and
unpretentiously, and therefore serenely, authentically and impressively, to express the good creation of God, which also in-
cludes the limitation and end of man?' (III,3, pp. 298-9).

We shall never truly understand the *Church Dogmatics* if
we forget Anselm, Calvin, and Wolfgang Amadeus Mozart.

There are great omissions from the chorus of voices which
make up the confessions of the Church. An Englishman may

grieve that Barth knew so little of, not just Anglican, but English theology in general. He mentions two or three from the past, Edward Irving (and he was a Scot!), Wesley, and the old Puritan lurking under the improbable disguise of "Purkins, Wilhelm". But there is only one ancient and one modern work that he quotes — *The Pilgrim's Progress* and Sir Edwyn Hoskyns' *The Fourth Gospel*. On the great English theologians like John Donne, Lancelot Andrewes, Richard Field, John Pearson, John Owen, J. H. Newman, P. T. Forsyth (another Scot) he is silent. Indeed, the present writer found in conversation that, although he knew Donne's poetry (the *Songs and Sonets*) he knew nothing of the sermons, and that Andrewes was not even a name to him — a great pity, for he would have found in Lancelot Andrewes a kindred spirit, and one whose so-called "metaphysical" style bore some resemblance to that of the *Church Dogmatics*. He would also have learned that there was a century when the Church of England did not despise systematic theology. The same gaps are apparent in Barth's knowledge of English literature. He knew the more obvious English novelists, liked Dickens, disapproved of D. H. Lawrence, and was appalled at *Brave New World*. He read omnivorously in detective novels; Dorothy Sayers was the best of all, he said (and indeed, he had translated one of her religious books into German). But had he known Shakespeare thoroughly, he would have found one who matched Mozart, not only in talent, but also in representing faithfully "the whole context of providence".

In the earlier writings, Matthias Grünewald had been cited for the outer leaf of his triptych painted as the altarpiece for the abbot's chapel in the monastery of Isenheim. No one who has seen these profound paintings in the museum Unter den Linden in Colmar, where they are now housed, could be unmoved by them or ever forget them. In some art galleries — say, the Frick in New York, or the Kunstmuseum in Basel — you are delighted again and again. In Colmar you are silenced. The outer panels portray the Crucifixion — the dying Christ with an unsparing horror of pain, despair, and putrefaction; the mother of Jesus supported by the beloved disciple; Mary Magdalen kneeling in frenzied prayer to Christ; and on the other side, John the Baptist, Bible open in his left hand and with his right pointing with lone forefinger to Christ, while at his feet stands a lamb bearing a cross and a chalice. This was what Barth fastened on in the early days, the witness of John the Baptist, a parable of the duty of the preacher and the theologian, to point steadfastly in one direction and in one only — to Jesus Christ.

Nor is this part of the triptych forgotten in the *Church Dogmatics*: 'The example of a Biblical witness in the unity of its form is John the Baptist . . . . In this connection one might recall John the Baptist in Grünewald's Crucifixion, especially his prodigious index finger: can any one point away from himself more impressively and completely . . . ? And can anyone point to the thing indicated more impressively and realistically, than is done here?' (I,1, p. 126).

But in the next volume the triptych is opened, to let us see the second pair of leaves, which depict the infant Jesus and his mother: 'There are three things to be seen in the picture, and it is difficult to say where the observer should begin. In the background upon the heights of heaven, beyond earth's highest mountains, surrounded by innumerable angels, there is God the Father in his glory. In the foreground to the left there is the sanctuary of the old covenant. It also is filled with and surrounded by angels, but inexorably separated from the background by an immensely high, gloomy partition. But towards the right a curtain is drawn back, affording a view. And at this point, at the head of the whole world of Advent looking to see the Messiah, stands Mary as the recipient of grace, the representative of all the rest, in adoration before what she sees happening on the right side. Over there, but quite lonely, the child Jesus lies in his mother's arms, surrounded by unmistakable signs reminding us that he is a child of earth like all the rest. Only this little child, not the mother, sees what is to be seen there, the Father. He alone, the Father, sees right into the eyes of this child. On the same side as the first Mary appears the Church, facing at a distance. It has open access on this side, it adores, it magnifies, and praises. Therefore, it sees what is indeed the glory of the only-begotten of his Father, full of grace and truth. But it sees only indirectly. What it sees directly is only the light that falls upon the Son, and the Son only in this light from the Father' (I,2, p. 125).

The *Church Dogmatics*, this faith seeking understanding, accepts just this condition. It keeps its gaze fixed steadfastly on the Incarnate Word, Jesus Christ. It will look for God only through him. It will look at him only as the Incarnate Word. And the glory of the *Church Dogmatics* consists precisely in the consistency and clear-sightedness with which it has accepted the condition and worked by it. From the Prolegomena through to the final Fragment which was published but the other day all doctrines are considered and shaped by these terms. Sometimes the treatment is direct, as in the knowledge of God, or the doctrine of man, or election; sometimes it is indirect and more subtle, as in the chapter on angels. Commonly it is executed with certainty and authority,. occasionally (say, the casting of the doctrine of the Mediator in terms of the Prodigal Son) it is unconvincing and even perverse. But always Barth's dogmatics strives to be the witness, pointing in the one direction. 'God is active in His Word; therefore dogmatics must remain bound to His Word, and can undertake only to give an account of that which is revealed in the Word of God as the past, present and future activity of God, of that which is an event in the Word, with all the force of what occurred yesterday, occurs today, and will occur tomorrow. And God's Word is His Son Jesus Christ. Therefore in the most comprehensive sense of the term dogmatics can and must be understood as Christology . . . . It must always remember that it can legitimately speak only of the God and the work and activity of the God who is the revelation of the Father in Jesus Christ by the Holy Spirit' (I,2, p. 883).

'Casting down imaginations, and every high thing that is exalted against the knowledge of God, and bringing every thought into captivity to the obedience of Christ' (2 Cor. 10.5).

CHAPTER EIGHT

Unfinished Work

THE WOODS DECAY, THE WOODS DECAY AND FALL; BUT THE WRITING of the *Church Dogmatics* strides onwards on its long journey. The decades pass; the situation of Barth himself and of the world at large changes and changes again; but the great volumes, draped in their robes of white like baptizands. of old, pass in regular succession through the water of public initiation to take their place in the company of the teachings of the doctors of the Church.

Within a year of the publication of I,1 'we were plunged into the Third Reich and the German Church-conflict. From that time the affairs of Europe and finally of the whole world hurtled with ever-increasing violence into the crisis which still engulfs us. By the very nature of things I have not been able to devote the last ten years solely to dogmatics, as was my intention in 1932. Yet dogmatics has been ever with me, giving me a constant awareness of what should be my central and basic theme as a thinker' (II,2, p. ix).

Barth has moved from his mid-forties to his late fifties. His university work continues, but now within a little country surrounded by the armies of the Nazis and living in fear of the fate that has befallen Holland, Belgium, Norway, Czechoslovakia, Austria. Under the threat of invasion there is formed an underground organization which would continue the struggle. Of this body Barth is a member, as he is also of the Swiss Home Guard. In these strained and distracting circumstances were written *The Doctrine of God* (1940 and 1942) and the first part of *The Doctrine of Creation* (1945).

Germany is destroyed and dismembered. Those of her rulers yet living are brought to justice. Russia and Communism seize command of Eastern Europe; the Communist bloc and America with her associates watch one another with continual suspicion;

the very peace is savage. The cold war at last yields place to apprehensive coexistence and ways are energetically, learnedly, and expensively sought to destroy larger and larger numbers of people at one blow.

Nevertheless, that day of rare felicity has dawned in Western Europe when you can think what you like and say what you think. Bonn makes the *amende honorable* for Barth's dismissal by at once inviting him back to lecture during the summer terms of 1946 and 1947. In the first year he lectures once more on the old Church document that has never failed to call out his highest powers, the Apostles' Creed. For the first time in his life he lectures extemporarily, but his words are taken down in short-hand and from this course there emerges the warmly evangelical *Dogmatics in Outline*.

Returning to Germany laid before Barth a choice. He had lived in that land for thirteen years. He had been a leading figure in the struggle of the Confessing Church. Now the Church, weakened by a decade of persecution and by the loss of some of her leaders, bewildered by the strange new gift of freedom which it hardly knew how to use, was in need of counsel and help. Was it now Barth's duty to return to Germany and devote the rest of his life to the reconstruction of that Church and indirectly of the country and of Europe? Against this stood only the *Church Dogmatics*. 'I felt that I ought to decide for the second' (*How I Changed*, p. 56).

Barth moves from his sixtieth birthday to his seventieth. He has become famous, one of the great Europeans. It is recognized that this theologian, who refuses to be anything but a theologian, has a peculiar contribution to make to contemporary European thought. That, in particular, his theological doctrine of man, far from echoing in religious language the customary anthropological doctrines of man, is genuinely new and therefore interesting to man himself, even to non-religious man. It becomes evident to others besides theologians that Barth's view that genuine humanity is to be found in the one man Jesus Christ, and that we may speak, not of the divinity of man, as the nineteenth century had done, but of the humanity of God, carries profound significance for man's life. He is awarded the

Danish Sonning Prize for exceptional contributions to European culture. He is invited to address the Goethe Society in Hanover. He is the guest speaker at the Basel Mozart celebrations in 1956. It is, however, as a theologian that he travels to England to be presented by the Archbishop of Canterbury with a copy of the British *Festschrift* in his honour at Lambeth Palace, and that he journeys to distant America to lecture at the Universities of Chicago and Princeton. But still the *Church Dogmatics* continues on its way. The three further parts of *The Doctrine of Creation* appear in 1948, 1950 and 1951. *The Doctrine of Reconciliation* makes a start in 1953 and is quickly followed up in 1955. But after this four years are to pass before the two parts of IV,3 are published in 1959.

All this while Barth had been quietly pursuing a ministry that he had by no means renounced when he changed from pastor to professor. It was with a book of sermons that he and Eduard Thurneysen began their career as authors, and this two years before *The Epistle to the Romans* appeared. They repeated their venture with *Come Holy Spirit* (1924), containing sermons from the last years at Safenwil and the first two or three at Göttingen, and, on Thurneysen's side, from Leutwil and Bruggen. No indication is given of the authorship of individual sermons, a deliberate anonymity proclaiming the all-importance of the Gospel, the insignificance of the preacher. When we investigate a little, we find that eleven sermons were by Thurneysen, fourteen by Barth. Among Barth's were no doubt the seven on II Corinthians, preached at Safenwil in 1920. He writes to Thurneysen (who has just moved to his new parish near St Gall) on May 31: 'The Second Letter to the Corinthians sweeps over me like a torrent. Only the smallest part can flow on in the way of sermons. The great If and But intrudes itself threateningly between *Paul* — and my speaking or the Safenwilers' hearing, and renders the whole light that shines in these texts (I am just at the fourth chapter) broken, conditional, one could also say churchly' (*Rev. Theol.* p. 51). And a fortnight later: 'I am doing my preparatory work on II Corinthians 5. That is indeed a chapter! If only one could succeed even a little in letting such passages speak once more' (p. 52). From Thurneysen, who made

the selection and edited the volume, we learn also that the three
sermons called 'The Great "But" ', 'The Name of the Lord', and
'The Small Moment' were preached by Barth in Göttingen.

These are not strictly expository sermons. True, Barth will
usually take as his text a passage of several verses and preach
about it; but he will not follow closely the movement of the
sentences and clauses in the manner of the older expository
preachers. Rather he will seize on the general meaning of the
passage, particularly as expressed in one striking phrase. Thus
the text of 'The Small Moment' is Isaiah 54.7-10, but, aside
from the first paragraph, the part of the text that forms the heart
of the sermon is the first verse: 'For a small moment have I
forsaken thee; but with great mercies will I gather thee'.

Those on II Corinthians, which presumably formed part of
a longer series and which were preached just before the revision of *The Epistle to the Romans*, usually pay closer attention to the text. Yet they do so in a specific way. They are the
sermon analogues to *The Epistle to the Romans*. With a minimum
of historical information they forthwith transpose this epistle into
modern life. Sometimes it is a direct word from Paul to the
Safenwil congregation. Such is the great sermon on Chapter 3.12-
17, entitled 'Moses-Time and Christ-Time'. The children of Israel, whose minds are hardened and over whose hearts hangs a
veil until they shall turn to the Lord, are the minister and his
congregation in their Swiss village church. "Unto this day" (vv.
14-15) refers to May, 1920. Moral standards have declined everywhere. The war has brought about the breakdown of the old,
settled order. Social injustice is heavy on the conscience of every
sensitive man. Now surely we need to assert more forcibly than
ever the necessity for high standards; now surely we need to
try to find our way back to the settled and secure world still
fresh in our memories; now surely we need to proclaim social
righteousness with all the force at our command. Now surely is
the age that needs the authority of Moses. 'All this we have
done. But what did it amount to? We have lighted candles in
the darkness . . . but the New Day has not dawned with them'
(p. 236). Moses-Time, necessary as it is, is not Christ-Time. To
Moses-Time belong demands and commands, awareness of guilt,

restitution. 'All these things you may do and perhaps you ought to do; but not enough has been done. For none of them atones for your sins; none of them clears the road . . . . If you go wrong here, it may well be that you are turning away from God by your very conversion' (p. 235). But Christ so transcends Moses that he passes away. Christ does not only command; he also bestows, he stoops to us, he gives life, he sets us free from our prison-house. Is not this age in reality crying out for men who know and believe this? It needs men who do not trust themselves but the God who makes all things new. It needs men who know what forgiveness is. There is plenty of Moses-zeal in the world, but there are few Christ-men. If we were to apply this to ourselves, the veil would have been lifted, Moses-Time would have passed away and Christ-Time begun.

The next volume of sermons appeared in 1935. *God's Search for Man* was published at the height of the German Church struggle; and indeed, the title page reflects Barth's interim state, for it refers to him as 'Former Professor of Theology in the University of Bonn, Germany'. Of these sermons I have been able to ascribe only five to their authors. From Thurneysen came 'The Mystery of the Gospel', 'Hosanna, Help!' and 'There shall be Signs' (all of which originally appeared in *Theologische Existenz heute*, 8). The two on the Good Shepherd are by Barth. (The second is, in fact, not a sermon at all but an address he gave at the Reformed Church Conference at Osnabrück on April 18, 1934). The first was preached at the Lutheran Church in the Rue Blanche in Paris on Sunday, April 15, 1934. It belongs to the same date as the Synod of Barmen, deals with the same subject as the beginning of the Declaration, and should be read in conjunction with it.

The most obvious difference between these sermons and the earlier volume is their greater clarity and order. They lose nothing of the former passion, but it is now easier to grasp the preacher's intention. Barth can hardly be said to have made listening easy for his Safenwil congregation, any more than he set an easy task for the readers of *The Epistle to the Romans*. 'Thirty years hence we may perhaps speak of simplicity,' he said austerely, 'but now let us speak the truth' (*Romans*, p. 5). Fortunately it

did not take him thirty years to arrive at a measure of simplicity in his preaching without sacrificing the truth.

By the time we reach the later years of the nineteen-fifties,
simplicity has been won. Nothing could be simpler, more direct,
more ordered than his sermons now. In form they differ somewhat from the earlier ones. Most of them have only a brief text
and the sermons themselves are little more than half the length
of those in days past. In their treatment of the text, however,
they are not much changed. They follow the movement of the
text, letting it speak in that devastatingly frank and childlike
way that Barth had. Was he not, indeed, something of a Prince
Muishkin, hearing without distrust and speaking without subter-
fuge?

It is October 7, 1956. Karl Barth is preaching in his local
church in Basel. His text is Leviticus 26.12: 'I will walk among
you, and will be your God, and you shall be my people'. The
doctrine of the covenant expressed in this verse holds a central
place in his theology, and the verse itself, or others like it, is
quoted frequently in the *Church Dogmatics*. Here he takes each
clause in succession to declare the reality and not simply the
potentiality of the promise contained in it. He treats the verse
in the anatomizing manner of Lancelot Andrewes. 'I will *walk*
among you': God walks; he is not static, he is the living God
who is on his way. 'I will walk *among* you': God walks along
our roads and in our houses and our places of work and recrea-
tion and in our churches; he is the God who is near at hand. 'I
will walk *among* you' means 'in your midst'; he is not simply on
the boundary of life, but is the centre, the source and the origin.
And this promise 'I will walk among you' is true independently
of our awareness of the fact. 'And I will be your God': I will
walk among you, not as an observer or an uninterested stranger,
but as the one who cares for you, who addresses you, who calls
you to obedience. I will be your partisan and helper, rescuing
you, supporting you, making you free and joyful. I speak to you
my good word which always has in it a health-giving rejection
of everything within you that harms you. 'And you shall be my
people': *God's* people — what an inconceivable and wonderful
privilege! 'And *you* shall be my people': not you when you have

become like the angels of God, but you in this life, you, just as you are. 'And you shall be my *people*': not just a collection of unrelated individuals, but a people of brothers and sisters.

This sermon occurs in *Deliverance to the Captives* (1959), a collection which, with *Call For God* (1965), takes us into an unexpected place, transports us in a sense back to the Safenwil days, even to the world of Dostoevsky, of *Crime and Punishment*. From about 1954 Barth visited Basel prison to preach in its chapel. He had been a village preacher, he had preached in city churches and cathedrals, he had preached over the radio. Now he was called upon to undertake this delicate task, where it would be only too easy to forfeit the good will of the congregation, where the twin temptations continually lurked of ignoring the special character of the congregation or of humiliating them. Barth speaks to them as a human being to fellow human beings. He accepts the fact that they are in prison, and is not afraid to refer to "prison" and "locked doors" and even "criminals". He can do this without embarrassment and indeed with a certain brotherliness, because he knows that there is something worse than being a criminal, and that is being a sinner — and that in this situation there is nothing to choose between them and himself. 'Let me tell you quite frankly: we are all together great sinners. Please understand me: I include myself. I stand ready to confess to being the greatest sinner among you all — but you must not then exclude yourself from the group! Sinners are people who in the judgment of God, and perhaps of their own consciences, have sinned and lost their way, who are not just a little but totally guilty, hopelessly indebted, and lost not only in time but in eternity. We are such sinners. Believe me, there is a captivity much worse than the captivity in this house. There are walls much thicker and doors much heavier than those closed upon you. . . . But now listen. Into the depth of our predicament the word is spoken from on high: *By grace you have been saved*. To be saved does not just mean to be a little encouraged, a little comforted, a little relieved. It means to be plucked out like a brand from a burning fire. You have been saved! We are not told: you may be saved sometimes, or a little bit. No, you *have been* saved, totally and for all time. You? Yes, we! Not just any other people, more pious and better than we are; no, we, each one of us' (*Deliverance*, p. 37).

Meanwhile the *Church Dogmatics*, like Robert Bridges' "Splendid ship", its "white sails crowding", had been scattering the foam before its prow. A quarter of a century had passed since its first appearance. Most theologians would feel that they had not spent an entirely idle twenty-seven years if in that time they had produced — inter alia! — twelve volumes totalling some nine thousand pages. Barth, however, was always presenting his apologies to the readers for his slowness. On his sixty-second birthday, in 1948, he wrote: 'This continuation of the *Church Dogmatics* . . . has not been able to appear according to plan. The outward cause of delay is that the summer terms of 1946 and 1947 — very busy times in other respects — were spent in Bonn, where I could not continue this work. The inward cause is that the theme [*The Creature*] involved a constant collecting, assessing and shaping of material before I dared publish the results' (III,2, p. ix). But Part 3 was out just two years later, and within another year Part 4.

Two years more and the first part of *The Doctrine of Reconciliation* makes its appearance. Barth can now quite happily report: 'I am still in good heart, and can devote myself to this great task . . . although the task is a heavy one, I do not have to stagger under its weight, but year in year out it carries me along with it. I now turn to it again. The way is long. But "having still time on the earth . . . " ' (IV,1, p. x).

Although only the customary two years separated the first two parts of this volume, increasing years had made the burden correspondingly heavier. The Foreword strikes a new note: 'I now have to accept without complaint or contradiction the fact that I am sometimes called "the old man in Basel", so I can only ask that I may have the indulgence of such if I fail to produce with the regularity of clockwork. I could not do this, indeed, even when I was younger. I can only say that I have the best will in the world to press on, but have been burdened with the responsibility of a task which this time was too much for me, and I found it impossible to finish it earlier' (IV,2, p. ix). 'When,' he said towards the end of the Foreword, 'will the next volume

appear? and how many more are there to be? — are questions
which I always hear soon after the publication of a new one.
And one student asked me, in a well-chosen phrase, what is
going to happen when "if I may be permitted to say so, you are
no longer there?" . . . "Fast falls the eventide" is only too true
of me, but I am still here and will address myself at once to
the next part' (IV,2, p. xii).

The next part, however, took longer than usual in coming.
It was still possible for him to lay the larger part of the responsibility on circumstances rather than on his inward resources.
One cause was the curtailing of the number of his lectures;
another the celebrations and travels which attended his seventieth
birthday. Yet it would seem that the impetus needed to carry
through the work was beginning to flag. Four years passed before
IV,3 appeared. And now in the Foreword Barth, well into his
seventies, looks back at the friends 'who have passed from the
present scene' — among them Arthur Frey, who had written
the good book on the German Church conflict, *Cross and Swastika*, and who, as director of Barth's publishers, had superintended
the publication of the *Church Dogmatics* for many years; Pierre
Maury, the French Reformed theologian; Karl Ludwig Schmidt,
the New Testament scholar; Hermann Hesse, one of those who
STAND, in the dedication of *Credo*; 'and also the Anglican bishop George Bell, an ecumenist without guile, who in the summer
of 1956 welcomed me in his palace in Chichester with a warmth
which I shall never forget' (IV,3, p. xiii).

The Fourth Part of Volume IV was then planned, and indeed the opening section at least was written before the summer
of 1960. But thereafter the work hung fire. Barth retired from
his Chair in Basel in March 1962 and so lost the stimulus provided by the need to give lectures. In 1964 his health deteriorated
and he was never truly well again. Although he still intended to
finish *The Doctrine of Reconciliation*, he allowed his attention
to be distracted from it first to an autobiography and then to the
Second Vatican Council, for the better understanding of which
he travelled to Rome in September 1966.

The promised final part of the *Church Dogmatics* failed for
so long to appear that it was commonly believed that the work

had now reached its end. But ~~in~~ mid-1967 there came out the slim Volume IV, Part 4, *Fragment: The Christian Life. Baptism as the Foundation of the Christian Life.* With this final portion the *Church Dogmatics* was, like the *Summa Theologica* of Thomas Aquinas, left incomplete.

The road trodden long since had led to the desert. And behold! the theological desert had rejoiced, and blossomed as the rose. It had blossomed abundantly, and rejoiced even with joy and singing: